Any Bitch's Husband Has To Cook™

And we *still* mean "Bitch" in a good way...
Babe **I**n **T**otal **C**ontrol of **H**erself

*Experience another
fun creation
brought to you by*

J. Wilde
San Angelo, TX

Published by J. Wilde

© Copyright 2003 by Pete Wilde

ISBN 0-9701502-1-0

Publication #9346

Printed in the United States of America by:

G & R Publishing Company
507 Industrial Street
Waverly, IA 50677
800-383-1679
gandr@gandrpublishing.com
http://www.cookbookprinting.com

Any Bitch's Husband Has To Cook . . .

If he is hungry . . .
or she is hungry . . .
or the kids are hungry . . .
or company is coming for dinner . . .

Because she is probably busy
working out . . .
or getting a facial . . .
or tanning . . .
or shopping . . .

Or (more likely)
She is working . . .
or taking care of the kids . . .
or volunteering . . .
or doing carpool . . .
or painting the brown paneling he had to have . . .
or scraping the acoustic off of the ceiling.

She isn't lazy; cooking just isn't at the top of her list.

But Any Bitch's Husband still has to cook . . .
If he plans to eat!

I

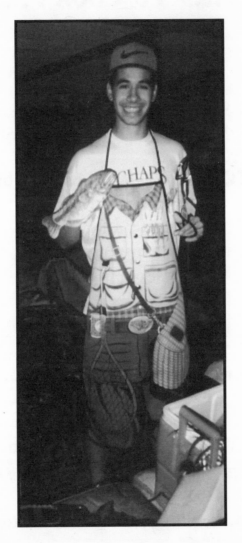

Brandon discovered true happiness
when he married a woman
who let him cook.

Dedication

This book is dedicated to all the wives
who allow their husbands to cook.
It can't be easy to stand back in your husband's shadow,
in his steam and smoke,
while he gets all the glory and attention
for having put a beautiful home-cooked meal on the table.
What would we husbands do with all our extra time
if we couldn't spend it cooking????

Pete Wilde

– Pete Wilde
Husband of Joyce Wilde

"Where's daddy?
I need my halftime snack!"

Women cook alone,
Men cook with their best friends.

My Favorite Recipes

RECIPE NAME   PAGE #

My Favorite Recipes

RECIPE NAME   PAGE #

My Favorite Recipes

RECIPE NAME   PAGE #

Table of Contents

Lookin' for a chef... in all the wrong places.

Appetizers & Drinks

AVOCADO DIP

1/2 C. mayonnaise
1/2 C. sour cream
2 T. lemon juice
1 peeled tomato, seeded and chopped
2 T. minced onion

Salt to taste
White pepper to taste, optional
2 medium ripe avocados, mashed
Dash garlic powder

Mix all ingredients together and serve with Fritos or crackers. Also good served on toast as a sandwich.

AVOCADO DIP

Lightly mash 4 avocados.

COMBINE WITH:
1 tsp. seasoned salt
2 T. lemon juice
1/8 tsp. Tabasco

1/2 tsp. Worcestershire
1 finely chopped tomato, medium

Chill before serving with chips or crackers.

BEAN DIP

1 can ranch style beans
1 can chili

1 can Ro-Tel tomatoes
1/2 lb. grated longhorn cheese

Blend in blender. Add 2 tablespoons flour. Cook until thick. Makes about 1 quart.

BEER NUTS

16 oz. raw peanuts
1/2 C. water

1 C. sugar

Mix together and boil for 15 minutes, keep stirring. Spread on cookie sheets; salt. Bake at 350° for 15 minutes. Mix. Turn off oven and let set for 15 minutes.

To love and honor are okay, the one might promise to obey.
But what makes husbands turn slowly gray,
is what to cook each blessed day.

CHEESE BALL

12 oz. Philadelphia cream cheese
6 oz. grated Cheddar cheese
1 T. grated onion

1 tsp. Worcestershire sauce
1 C. ground pecans

Combine cheeses, onions, and sauce in a medium size bowl; beat in 1/2 cup pecans. Shape into ball; roll in remaining nuts. Cover and refrigerate. Optional: May add green peppers or olives.

CHEESE OLIVE PUFFS

1/4 lb. sharp cheese, grated
1/4 C. margarine
1/2 C. flour

1/2 tsp. paprika
1/4 tsp. salt
24 small stuffed olives

To grated cheese, add margarine and blend well. Sift flour. Measure flour and resift with salt and paprika. Add to cheese. Wrap 1 teaspoonful of dough around each olive. Bake 12 minutes at 400°. This should make exactly 24 cheese puffs. They can be made ahead of time and kept in refrigerator until ready to bake.

CHEESE SPREAD

1 lb. Velveeta
8 oz. cream cheese
1/2 C. Western dressing
1/2 C. mayonnaise or Miracle Whip

1 small bunch green onions
1 green pepper
2 pkgs. dried beef

Melt Velveeta (this works great in the microwave). With electric mixer, beat cream cheese until softened. Mix in Western dressing and mayonnaise. Add melted Velveeta and beat until smooth and creamy. Chop green onions, green pepper, and dried beef. Combine with cheese mixture (do not use electric mixer). Serve spread with crackers.

*Intelligence is like a river –
the deeper it flows, the less noise it makes.*

CANDIED CHICKEN WINGS

3 lbs. chicken wings
Salt and pepper to taste
1/2 tsp. paprika
1/2 C. honey

1/4 C. soy sauce
4 T. brown sugar
1 crushed clove garlic
1/4 C. ketchup

Place cleaned and disjointed chicken wings in foil-lined 9x13" pan. Sprinkle with salt, pepper and paprika. Combine honey, soy sauce, brown sugar, garlic and ketchup. Pour over chicken and bake at 400° for 1 hour, uncovered, turning and basting every 15 minutes with sauce mixture. Serves 10 to 12. Very tasty!

COCKTAIL WIENERS

1 1/2 lbs. cocktail wieners
1 jar mustard

1 jar currant jelly

Place all in crock pot and put on low for a couple of hours.

CRAB DIP

1 1/4 C. mayonnaise
1 C. shredded crab meat
1/2 C. finely grated Cheddar cheese

1 tsp. horseradish
4 T. French dressing
Grated onion to taste

Mix all of the above, adding onion to suit taste. French dressing and horseradish can be increased also. Best to make several hours ahead of time. Serve with crackers.

CREAM CHEESE DIP

8 oz. cream cheese, softened
1 T. minced onion
1 T. French dressing

1 T. milk
1/4 tsp. garlic salt
1/3 C. ketchup

Mix well and refrigerate.

It costs nothing to say something nice about someone.

DEVILED HAM DIP

1-6 3/4 oz. can Underwood deviled
  ham
1-8 oz. pkg. softened cream cheese

1/2 to 1 tsp. garlic powder
2 to 3 T. Hellmann's mayonnaise

Soften cream cheese. Blend in deviled ham. Add garlic powder and enough mayonnaise to make it smooth. May add 1 ounce chopped pimento, 1/2 tablespoon Worcestershire sauce, 2 tablespoons grated onion, 2 tablespoons pickle juice or ketchup for more variety.

EIGHT LAYER DIP

1-10 1/4 oz. can jalapeno bean dip
1-6 3/4 oz. container avocado dip
1 C. dairy sour cream
4 oz. (1 C.) shredded Cheddar cheese

4 oz. (1 C.) shredded brick or Monterey
  Jack cheese
1 C. chopped green onions
2 tomatoes, chopped
1-5 oz. can sliced black olives, drained

On a 12" to 14" serving plate or platter, spread bean dip to about 3/8" thickness. Carefully spread avocado dip on bean dip to within 3/4" of edge. Spoon sour cream on avocado dip to within 3/4" of previous edge. Top with remaining ingredients, arranging in concentric circles. Cover and chill. Serve with crackers or corn chips. Makes 12 to 15 servings.

EGG ROLLS

1 lb. hamburger or any kind of meat
2 medium onions
1 T. salt
4 C. shredded cabbage

1 C. chopped celery
1 pkg. fresh bean sprouts
1/4 C. soy sauce
1 pkg. egg roll wraps

Fry meat; drain grease. Add all of the other ingredients. Cook until vegetables are limp; drain in strainer for several hours. Take egg roll wraps and put 1 tablespoon or so of mixture on edge. Moisten other edge with water; roll it up. Fry in oil, turning as it browns. Mixture will keep in refrigerator for a week or so.

If you don't have time to do it right,
when are you going to find the time to do it over?

GOLDEN CHEESE SPREAD

2 C. shredded sharp Cheddar
  cheese
1-3 oz. pkg. cream cheese
1/2 C. mayonnaise

1/2 tsp. Worcestershire
1/8 tsp. onion salt
1/8 tsp. garlic salt
1/8 tsp. celery salt
2 oz. jar diced pimentos

Mix all ingredients together. This is a quick and easy spread for crackers or vegetables.

HOMEMADE SALAMI

2 to 2 1/2 lbs. good ground beef
1/2 tsp. onion powder
1/2 tsp. garlic powder
2 T. curing salt (Tender-Quick)

1 T. mustard seed
1 1/2 tsp. liquid smoke
Pinch of crushed red pepper
3/4 C. water

Mix all together. Shape into 3 rolls on foil and wrap. Refrigerate for 24 hours. Open up foil and bake at 300° for 1 hour and 15 minutes.

JALAPENO PEPPERS

1 lb. jalapeno peppers
1-8 oz. pkg. cream cheese, softened
1/8 C. minced onion

1/3 C. grated Cheddar cheese
1 lb. bacon slices
Seasoning salt to taste

Cut jalapeno peppers in halves longways. Devein, removing all seeds. Mix together cream cheese, onion, cheese, and seasoning salt. Fill jalapenos with cream cheese mixture, without heaping. Cut bacon slices into 3 pieces. Wrap jalapenos with bacon and use toothpick to hold. Place on foil or rack and grill for approximately 45 minutes. Hotness will disappear!

ONION BAKE

White bread
Finely chopped onion

Parmesan cheese
Mayonnaise

Remove crust from bread. Cut bread into rounds with a biscuit cutter and lightly toast. Spread with mayonnaise; top with chopped onion and Parmesan cheese. Broil until light brown around edges. Very easy and delicious appetizer.

PARTY MIX

2 C. Rice Chex
2 C. Corn Chex
2 C. Wheat Chex
2 C. Cheerios or Kix
1 small box pretzels
1 small jar mixed nuts (can use more)

2 cubes oleo
3 to 4 T. Worcestershire sauce
5 to 6 drops Tabasco sauce
3 tsp. garlic powder
3 tsp. onion powder
Salt

Melt oleo, Worcestershire sauce, Tabasco sauce, garlic powder and onion powder all together. Place the Chex, Cheerios, pretzels and nuts together in a very large roaster pan. Pour the oleo over the dry mixture; stir carefully and salt to taste. Place in 250° oven and bake for 1 to 1 1/2 hours, stirring every 10 to 15 minutes. Be sure to stir because it burns easily. When taken out of oven, place on absorbent paper and cool. Store in an airtight container.

RINA'S DIP

1/2 lb. hamburger
1/2 lb. breakfast sausage
1 can Ro-Tel tomatoes with green
 chilies

1 can cream of mushroom soup
1 pkg. onion soup mix (1 pkg. out of
 box)
16 slices American cheese

Cook hamburger and sausage until done; drain. In a separate pot, mash tomatoes and bring to a slow boil. Add cheese, 1 or 2 slices at a time. Stir as cheese melts to prevent sticking. After all cheese has melted, add mushroom soup, then onion soup mix. Put mixture in crock pot. Add hamburger and sausage to mixture in crock pot, while stirring. Add hot sauce to taste.

STUFFED MUSHROOMS

1 pkg. fresh mushrooms
2 slices dried bread crumbs

1 tsp. garlic salt
1/4 C. melted margarine

Wash mushrooms. Remove stems from the caps of the mushrooms. Save half the stems and chop into fine pieces. In a bowl, mix chopped stems, bread crumbs, salt and melted butter until all is moistened. Stuff caps with mixture and place on a baking sheet. Broil until golden brown.

STUFFED MUSHROOMS

18 medium fresh mushrooms
Melted butter

1-3 oz. pkg. softened cream cheese
1/2 C. grated Parmesan cheese

Remove stems and wipe mushrooms gently with damp cloth. Brush inside and out with melted butter. Mix cream cheese and Parmesan cheese together. Stuff into mushroom caps. Arrange on buttered baking sheet with cheese side up. Bake at 350° until lightly browned, 12 to 15 minutes. Serve immediately. Serves 6.

STUFFED CELERY

1 large pkg. cream cheese at room
  temp.
1/2 C. pecans, chopped
1/2 medium onion, minced

Approximately 20 diced, stuffed olives
Garlic salt to taste
Pepper to taste

Mix all ingredients in a bowl, then stuff in celery stalks that have been cut into 3" pieces. Chill before serving.

STUFFED JALAPENOS

2 cans whole jalapenos
1 small pkg. Philadelphia cream
  cheese

2 jars English sharp Cheddar cheese

Wash hot green jalapenos in hot water several times, then set in cold water, covered, overnight. Dry peppers; put mixed cream cheese and room temperature Cheddar cheese with a little mayonnaise, very small amount of garlic powder and small amount of finely chopped pecans into each half pepper. Keep cold until ready for use.

SPINACH DIP

1-10 oz. pkg. frozen spinach
1 pkg. Knorr vegetable soup mix
1 1/2 C. sour cream

1 C. mayonnaise
1-8 oz. can water chestnuts, chopped
3 green onions, chopped

Thaw spinach and squeeze dry. Stir soup mix, sour cream and mayonnaise until blended. Stir in spinach, water chestnuts and green onions. Cover; chill 2 hours. Stir before serving. Makes 4 cups.

TACO DIP

1ST LAYER:
1 lb. hamburger, precooked
1 can refried beans
1 pkg. taco seasoning

2ND LAYER:
8 oz. pkg. cream cheese
1/2 jar taco sauce
3RD LAYER:
Shredded cheese

Bake until cheese melts.

TACO DIP

1 container sour cream
2-8 oz. cream cheese
1 packet taco seasoning
2 C. shredded Cheddar cheese

1 ripe tomato, diced
Black olives, diced
1 head lettuce
Tortilla chips

Mix sour cream, cream cheese and taco seasoning mix in small bowl with a hand mixer until well blended. Then take a spatula and spread this mixture onto a glass platter or serving tray. Add shredded lettuce on top of this mixture. Top with cheese, tomatoes and black olives. Serve immediately with chips or refrigerate until serving time.

TORTILLA ROLLS

8 oz. cream cheese
8 oz. sour cream
8 oz. shredded Cheddar cheese

1 small can diced black olives, drained
1 small can green chilies, diced
1 pkg. flour tortillas

Combine and spread on flour tortilla. Roll up. Refrigerate and then slice. Great for parties.

TORTILLA PINWHEELS

2-8 oz. pkgs. cream cheese
1/4 to 1/2 C. sour cream
1-4 oz. can mild chopped green
  chilies
8 slices bacon, cooked and crumbled

6 green onions, chopped
1 C. bell pepper, chopped
1-4 oz. jar diced pimentos
2 tsp. seasoned salt
6 to 8 large flour tortillas

Mix cream cheese and sour cream until smooth. Add remaining ingredients and stir until well blended. Spread mixture on tortillas and roll up as a jelly roll. Chill. Slice into 1/2" slices (an electric knife works best). Makes 8 to 9 dozen.

TORTILLA PINWHEELS

1-8 oz. sour cream
1-8 oz. cream cheese
1-4 oz. can green chilies, chopped
1-4 oz. can black olives, diced
1 C. grated Cheddar cheese

1/2 C. chopped onions
Garlic powder
Seasoning salt
5 to 6-10" flour tortillas

Mix together all ingredients except tortillas. Spread evenly over tortillas and roll as tightly as possible. Wrap in foil or plastic wrap and chill at least 2 to 3 hours. Slice and serve with salsa.

SPINACH TORTILLA BITES

2-10 oz. pkgs. frozen, chopped
   spinach, thawed and well drained
6 green onions, chopped
1 pkg. ranch-style salad dressing mix

1 C. mayonnaise
1 jar bacon bits (not imitation)
1 C. sour cream
10 large flour tortillas

Mix together spinach, onions, dressing mix, mayonnaise, bacon bits and sour cream. Spread on tortillas; roll to enclose filling. Place on cookie sheet, seam side down. Wrap in plastic wrap and chill overnight. Slice into bite-size pieces, about 1/2". Let stand at room temperature for 15 minutes before serving.

THREE CHEESE SPREAD

1/4 lb. Monterey Jack cheese
1/4 lb. sharp Cheddar cheese
1/4 lb. Velveeta cheese
1/2 pt. mayonnaise
1 T. granulated sugar
1 T. salad mustard

1 dash Tabasco sauce
1-4 oz. jar diced pimentos
1/2 chopped onion
1/2 chopped bell pepper
Garlic salt to taste
Salt to taste

Grate the cheeses and mix together. Add mayonnaise, sugar, salad mustard and Tabasco sauce. Mix in the rest of the ingredients and blend well. Delicious cracker spread. Keeps for 2 to 3 weeks.

You can't change the past,
but you can ruin a perfectly good present
by worrying about the future.

MOCHA MIX

2 C. sugar
2 C. instant dry milk
2 C. Coffee-mate

1 C. cocoa (not cocoa mix)
1/2 C. instant coffee

Mix together and store in airtight container. Heat a cup of milk. Add 3 heaping tablespoons of mix and stir to blend. Adjust amount of mix for desired strength. Mix keeps indefinitely.

EASY RED PUNCH

1-46 oz. can cherry Hi-C.
1-46 oz. can red Hawaiian Punch

1-46 oz. can pineapple juice
1-28 oz. bottle ginger ale or 7-Up

Mix above ingredients all together.

HOMEMADE BRANDY

1 fifth vodka
2 C. sugar

4 C. berries (almost any fruit will work,
    red raspberries work very well,
    peaches (sliced), strawberries,
    cherries, etc.
Gallon jar

Put the ingredients in the gallon jar and use a lid that won't leak. Start with the jar right side up; then turn upside down the next day. Alternate this way for 2 weeks. Strain and bottle. The longer it sets, the better it gets. Yields 1 fifth and 1 pint.

VODKA SLUSH

1-12 oz. frozen orange juice
1-6 oz. frozen lemonade
1 C. sugar

1 C. brewed tea
5 C. boiling water

Mix this up and cool. Add 1 pint vodka. Freeze overnight.
TO SERVE: Fill glass 1/2 full of slush and the rest with 7-Up.

WEDDING PUNCH

1 qt. unsweetened pineapple juice
1 qt. orange juice
2 qts. sherbet (raspberry)

1 1/2 qts. ginger ale
1 qt. apple juice

Chill all juices before mixing. Combine juices, adding ginger ale last. Add sherbet just before serving.

ICED TEA

3 qts. boiling water
2 heaping T. loose tea

1 C. sugar
1 lemon

Steep tea and water for 3 minutes. While hot, add sugar and juice of the lemon. Cool for 2 hours. Strain.

PERFECT ICE TEA

Bring 1 quart water to a boil: Put 2 Lipton family size tea bags in the boiling water. Set aside and let cool at least 30 minutes. To make tea, mix the brewed tea in a pitcher with 1 1/2 quarts of cool water. Add 2/3 cup pure cane sugar and juice of 1/2 to 1 lemon, depending on what you like. Stir and enjoy. Makes a perfect tea every time. (You must let the boiled tea sit at least 30 minutes.)

LEMONADE

2 C. sugar
1 C. water
Rind of 2 lemons, cut into thin strips
1/8 tsp. salt

Juice of 6 lemons
6 qts. water
Lemon slices

Boil sugar, 1 cup water, lemon rind and salt for 5 minutes. Cool and add lemon juice; strain. Combine syrup and 6 quarts of water, or less, according to taste. Freeze lemon slices in ring mold. Add to punch bowl with lemonade.

People are lonely because they build walls instead of bridges.

VEGETABLE DIP

3/4 C. sugar
3 tsp. vegetable oil
6 tsp. mustard

1 1/2 C. salad dressing
3/4 tsp. garlic salt

Mix and let stand 1 hour before serving.

FRUIT DIP

8 oz. cream cheese

Small jar marshmallow creme

Mix together and use as a dip for fresh fruit.

VEGETABLE DIP

1 pt. sour cream
1 pt. salad dressing or mayonnaise
3 T. dill weed

1 T. onion flakes
2 tsp. parsley flakes

Mix all ingredients and refrigerate for 2 to 3 hours before serving.

You cannot help people permanently
by doing for them what they could
and should do for themselves.

Welcome to the family...
now please cook dinner!

Breads,
Sweet
Breads
& Brunch

BANANA BREAD

1/2 C. shortening	2 C. flour
1 C. sugar	1 tsp. soda
2 eggs	1 C. milk
2 medium bananas, mashed	1/2 C. chopped walnuts or pecans

Cream shortening and sugar. Add 1 egg at a time and beat. Blend in bananas. Sift and measure flour and soda. Add alternately with milk and flour. Add nuts. Mix well. Pour in greased loaf pan and bake 1 1/2 hours at 350°.

BANANA BREAD

BEAT WELL:

2 eggs	1 tsp. salt
2 tsp. baking powder	1 T. vanilla
1/2 tsp. soda	

BEAT WELL AND ADD TO ABOVE:

1 C. shortening	1 C. sugar
5 ripe bananas, mashed	

Add 2 1/2 cups flour and 2 teaspoons baking powder, sifted together. Mix well. Pour into ring pan. Bake at 250° for 55 to 60 minutes until done. Check with toothpick.

BEER BREAD

3 C. self-rising flour	1-12 oz. can warm beer (not light)
2 T. sugar	

Mix all together. Bake at 350° for 45 minutes in greased loaf pan. Remove from pan and coat with butter.

BEER BISCUITS

4 C. biscuit mix (any brand)	1-16 oz. can of beer, room temp.
2 T. sugar	

Mix together and pour into greased muffin tins. Place in oven preheated to 350° for 12 to 15 minutes or until biscuits are golden brown.

STANDARD BISCUIT

2 C. flour
1/2 tsp. salt
3 tsp. baking powder

3 to 4 T. shortening
2/3 to 3/4 C. milk

Sift flour with salt and baking powder; cut in shortening until mixture resembles coarse crumbs. Add milk all at once and mix just until dough follows fork around the bowl. Turn out on lightly floured board; knead gently 1/2 minute. Roll or pat 1/2" thick and cut with biscuit cutter. Bake on ungreased cookie sheet in hot oven at 450° for 12 to 15 minutes. Makes 16 medium sized biscuits.

BLUEBERRY BREAD

3/4 C. sugar
1/4 C. oleo
1 egg
1/2 C. milk

2 C. flour
2 tsp. baking soda
1/4 tsp. salt
2 C. blueberries

Mix all the ingredients, except the blueberries. Fold in the berries. Pour into greased baking dish.

Top with this mixture:
1/2 C. sugar
1/3 C. flour

1/2 tsp. cinnamon
1/4 C. butter

Bake at 375° for 50 minutes or more.

BLUEBERRY MUFFINS

1 egg
1 C. milk
1/4 C. oil
2 C. flour

1/2 C. sugar
3 tsp. baking powder
1 tsp. salt
1 C. frozen or fresh blueberries

Preheat oven to 400°. Stir all ingredients until flour is moistened. Batter should be lumpy. Do not overmix. Fill greased muffin tins 2/3 full. Bake for 20 to 25 minutes. Makes 12 muffins.

HOME BAKED BREAD

2 C. lukewarm water	1 1/2 T. salt
1 yeast cake or 1 pkg. dry yeast (2 if using whole wheat flour)	1 1/2 T. sugar
	Flour

Combine water, yeast, salt and sugar and mix well. When dissolved, add enough flour to make a stiff dough. Knead 5 minutes; let rise until double in bulk. Break off pieces of dough to form large rolls or small loaves, 6" or 8" long. Score diagonally with knife; brush with water. Put in greased loaf pan. Allow to set 30 minutes. Preheat oven to 400° F. and set a pan of water in it. Put bread dough in oven on rack above the water and bake about 30 minutes or until lightly browned.

BREAD IN A JAR

3 C. sugar	2 tsp. baking soda
1 C. vegetable oil	1 1/2 tsp. grated cinnamon
4 eggs	1 tsp. ground cloves
2 C. cooked, mashed sweet potatoes	1 1/2 tsp. allspice
2/3 C. water	1 1/2 C. golden raisins
3 1/2 C. all-purpose flour	1 1/2 C. chopped pecans
1 tsp. salt	8 wide-mouth pt. canning jars
1/2 tsp. baking powder	

Wash and rinse jars and rings; let dry. Grease jars with shortening. About 15 minutes before bread is ready to bake, place lids and rings in boiling water. Do not boil, but leave in hot water until ready to use. In a large bowl with electric mixer, blend sugar and oil. Add eggs and beat well. Add sweet potatoes and water. Sift together flour, salt, baking powder, soda, cinnamon, cloves and allspice. Add to sweet potato mixture. Mix on low until well mixed. Stir in raisins and pecans. Pour 1 cup plus 1 tablespoon of batter into each jar. Wipe off any batter that might be on the edge of the jar. Place jars on cookie sheet. Bake in preheated oven at 325° for 45 to 55 minutes. When done, remove jars from oven immediately, one at a time. If bread has risen above the top of the jar's edge, cut off excess. Wipe edge of jar clean and seal with scalded lid and ring. Let jars set until sealed. You will hear them pop. Turn upside down and cool. Bread will come loose from the sides and bottom. To serve, slice and serve as is or with whipped topping.

We may live without friends,
We may live without books,
But civilized women cannot live without cooks.

EASY CINNAMON ROLLS

2 pkgs. (24 count) dinner rolls
1-3 3/4 oz. pkg. butterscotch
  pudding mix (not instant)
1/2 C. butter

3/4 C. brown sugar
3/4 T. cinnamon
1/2 C. chopped nuts

Arrange rolls in greased tube pan. Sprinkle dry pudding mix over rolls. Cook butter and remaining ingredients over low heat until sugar is dissolved and mixture bubbles; pour over rolls. Cover tightly with foil and let stand overnight. Bake at 350° for 30 minutes. Let stand 5 minutes; invert onto serving dish.

COMPANY CORN BREAD

2 eggs
1-8 oz. can creamed corn, yellow or
  white

1 C. sour cream
1 C. self-rising white or yellow
  cornmeal

Beat eggs in bowl. Fold in corn, sour cream and cornmeal. Mix until blended. Bake in well-greased 8x8" pan at 400° for 25 minutes until brown. If you like the top browner, put under broiler for a few extra minutes. Brush with butter. Serve hot. Serves 6 to 8.

JELLO ROLLS

2 loaves frozen bread dough
1/2 stick melted margarine

TOPPING:
1/2 C. sugar
1/4 C. brown sugar
1 pkg. strawberry jello
3/4 tsp. cinnamon

Cut frozen bread dough in pieces after letting thaw overnight in refrigerator. Put in 9x13" pan. Mix topping together and sprinkle over dough. Top with 1/2 stick margarine. Let rise. Bake at 350° for 30 to 35 minutes. Drizzle with powdered sugar frosting.

Every story has three sides - yours, mine and the facts.

DROP DOUGHNUTS

5 1/2 C. flour
4 tsp. baking powder
1 1/4 C. sugar
1 tsp. nutmeg
1/2 tsp. cloves
1 tsp. cinnamon

2 tsp. salt
3 eggs
1 1/2 C. milk
2 tsp. vanilla
6 T. melted shortening
Granulated sugar

Mix all ingredients together and store in refrigerator. Fry fresh in oil as needed. The dough will keep up to 2 weeks.

TO FRY: Drop dough by teaspoons into hot fat at 365° to 375° and fry until browned, about 1 1/2 minutes. Drain on paper towels. Roll in sugar. Enjoy!

FRENCH CHEESE BREAD

1 large loaf French bread
1/2 C. mayonnaise
1/2 C. margarine
1 C. black olives, chopped

2 C. mozzarella cheese
2 cloves garlic, crushed
6 green onions, chopped

Add mayonnaise to margarine to soften. Once to a good mixture, add other ingredients; spread on bread already cut lengthwise. Bake at 350° for 15 to 20 minutes or until cheese is melted. Freezes well.

*People who light up your life
usually know where the switch is.*

KOLACHES

1 medium potato
3 C. milk
3 eggs, beaten
1 C. sugar
3 tsp. salt
1 tsp. cinnamon

1/2 tsp. nutmeg
2 pkgs. dry yeast
1/4 C. warm water
1 tsp. sugar
3/4 C. lard, melted
3 full sifters (12 C.) flour

Boil potato in 1/2 cup water. Pour off to 1/4 cup water. Mash potato and reserve. Add 3 cups milk to potato water and heat until it steams. Remove from heat. Add 1 cup sugar, salt, cinnamon and nutmeg. Add mashed potato to mixture. Stir in eggs. In another bowl, stir until smooth yeast, 1/4 cup warm water and 1 teaspoon sugar; add to egg mixture. Add 3/4 cup lard. Add sifted flour gradually and beat. Cover; let rise 1 1/2 hours. When it fills pan, beat down with a spoon. Add 1 teaspoon of lard, work with fingers, cover and let rise again. Roll out dough to 1/4" thick; cut into squares. Drop a teaspoon of mixture on each square. Fold like baby diapers. Put on greased cake pans; let rise. Bake at 400° for 12 to 15 minutes. Brush with butter after baking. Makes approximately 6 dozen.

PRUNE MIXTURE:
2 oz. pitted prunes

Cover with water; let boil until soft. Drain and mash with 1/2 to 3/4 cup sugar; mix well. Add dash of cinnamon to taste.

MONKEY BREAD

3 cans Pillsbury biscuits
1 C. sugar
2 tsp. cinnamon

1 C. brown sugar
1 stick oleo
Chopped nuts

Cut biscuits into fourths. Shake biscuits in a bag with granulated sugar and cinnamon. Layer biscuits in tube pan. Sprinkle chopped nuts between layers. Melt brown sugar and oleo; boil 1 minute. Pour over biscuits. Bake at 350° for 35 minutes. Let stand 10 minutes before removing from pan.

Duty is a matter of the mind.
Commitment is a matter of the heart.

PUMPKIN BREAD

3 C. sugar   1 C. oleo

Cream together.

ADD:
4 eggs	1/3 C. water
1 1/2 tsp. salt	2 C. pumpkin
1 tsp. cinnamon	3 2/3 C. flour
1/4 tsp. nutmeg	2 tsp. soda
	Chopped nuts, optional

Mix together. Bake in 2-9x5" greased and floured loaf pans at 350° for 1 hour.

QUICK AND EASY YEAST ROLLS

1 pkg. yeast	1/2 tsp. salt
3/4 C. warm water	1 egg
2 T. sugar	2 1/2 to 2 3/4 C. flour
2 T. vegetable oil	Soft butter

Dissolve yeast in water. Add sugar, oil, salt and egg. Stir. Add 1 cup flour. Let rise 15 minutes. Stir down batter; add 1 1/2 cups flour. Knead 3 minutes. If sticky, add 1/4 cup flour. Roll into 16 balls. Put in greased square pan 9x9x2". Brush tops with butter. Cover. Let rise 25 minutes. Bake at 425° for 12 to 15 minutes. Makes 16 rolls.

ZUCCHINI BREAD

3 eggs	1 C. salad oil
2 C. sugar	2 C. grated zucchini
1 tsp. vanilla	

Mix well together in large bowl.

SIFT TOGETHER:
3 C. flour	1 tsp. salt
1 tsp. baking soda	1/2 tsp. baking powder
1 tsp. cinnamon	

Add to squash mixture. Mix in 2/3 cup nuts. Divide mixture into 2 floured and greased bread pans. Bake at 325° for 1 hour and 15 minutes.

19

CAMP EGGS

8 eggs, well beaten
2 medium onions, finely chopped
1 green pepper, finely chopped
1/4 C. olive oil
1 clove garlic, crushed

1/2 tsp. salt
1/4 tsp. pepper
2 tsp. chili powder
1/4 tsp. oregano
1/2 tsp. comino powder

In skillet, sauté garlic in olive oil. Add onions and green pepper and sauté until soft. Add seasonings. Mix together; then add eggs and scramble until done. May be served wrapped in tortillas.

MEXICAN EGGS

1 pkg. tortillas
5 oz. longhorn cheese
5 to 6 eggs

SAUCE:
1 whole can chopped tomatoes
1 onion
1 can green chilies

To make sauce, sauté onions; add tomatoes and chilies. Let thicken. Cut tortillas in strips and fry until real crisp. Drain. Then add chips to sauce and let combination start to boil. Beat eggs and add to sauce and stir until eggs are cooked. Add cheese and stir until melted. If sauce gets too thick, add another can of tomatoes. Serve with refried beans and guacamole.

FRENCH TOAST

2 eggs
1 C. milk or buttermilk
2 tsp. sugar
1/2 tsp. vanilla

1/4 tsp. salt
8 slices firm bread
Butter

In a shallow bowl, beat eggs with a fork. Stir in milk, sugar, vanilla and salt. Dip bread into milk and egg mixture, coating both sides well. Melt butter in a large skillet; add bread and fry until golden brown on both sides.

The only fair way to talk about people
is to speak as though you knew they were listening in.

GARLIC JALAPENO GRITS

Cook 1 cup grits according to package directions.

TO HOT GRITS ADD:

2 T. butter
1 well-beaten egg
1 roll garlic cheese
1 roll jalapeno cheese

1 can green chilies, chopped
2 T. minced onions
Tabasco and cayenne to taste

Mix well and put in 2-quart casserole and bake 1 hour in 350° oven.

CHEESE GRITS CASSEROLE

MIX TOGETHER:

4 C. water
1 tsp. salt

1 C. grits, cooked

ADD:

1 stick oleo
4 oz. Velveeta cheese

4 oz. jalapeno cheese
2 eggs, well beaten

Mix well. Pour in lightly buttered casserole dish. Bake at 350° until set, about 40 to 50 minutes.

COWBOY OMELET

6 slices bacon, diced
2 T. finely chopped onion
1 C. grated raw potatoes
6 eggs, slightly beaten

1/2 tsp. salt
1/8 tsp. white pepper
Dash of hot sauce
2 T. minced parsley

Fry bacon until crisp; drain all but 2 tablespoons drippings from skillet. Sauté onion until soft in reserved drippings; add potatoes and cook until light brown. Pour eggs into skillet; add salt, pepper and hot sauce. Lift up edges with spatula to let uncooked egg mixture slide underneath. When firm, sprinkle with crumbled bacon and parsley. Fold omelet in half; serve immediately. Serves 4 to 6.

CORNMEAL PANCAKES

1 1/3 C. white or yellow cornmeal
1 1/4 tsp. salt

1/2 tsp. soda
1/2 C. sifted flour

Put above ingredients in a bowl.

ADD:
1/4 C. butter

Blend with a pastry blender.

COMBINE:
2 C. buttermilk

2 eggs

Stir into butter mixture with a few strokes. Beat between spoonings. Can set awhile.
SYRUP FOR PANCAKES: Heat slowly 1 cup honey and 1/2 cup maple syrup. Remove
from heat and add 1 teaspoon cinnamon.

FAVORITE PANCAKES

1 1/4 C. sifted all-purpose flour
3 tsp. baking powder

1 T. sugar
1/4 tsp. salt

Stir or sift together.

COMBINE:
1 beaten egg
1 C. milk plus a little more

2 T. salad oil

Mix with dry ingredients. Rub oil on hot griddle and cook. Flip when bubbles in
batter quit appearing.

Kindness, like a boomerang, always returns.

QUICHE FOR REAL MEN

1 ready-made pie crust
4 eggs
1/2 C. cream
Dash Worcestershire sauce
1/4 tsp. garlic salt

1-10 oz. can cream of celery soup
1/2 lb. bacon, cooked and crumbled
1 C. diced broccoli
1-4 oz. can mushrooms
1/2 lb. Swiss cheese, grated

Preheat oven to 325°. Prepare pie crust per package directions. In a mixing bowl, beat together eggs and cream until frothy. Stir in Worcestershire and garlic salt. Using a whisk, or mixer on low speed, mix in soup a little at a time until all soup is added and the mixture is smooth. Spread the crumbled bacon over the pie crust. Then add the broccoli, mushrooms and cheese, tossing to combine. Pour the soup mixture over all to fill the pie shell. Bake uncovered for 1 hour or until firm in the center.

CHEESE SAUSAGE QUICHE

1 lb. bulk sausage
1/2 C. onion, chopped
1/3 C. green pepper, chopped
1/2 C. sharp Cheddar cheese, grated
1 T. flour
2 eggs, beaten
1 C. evaporated milk

1 T. parsley or 1 tsp. dehydrated parsley flakes
3/4 tsp. seasoned salt
1/4 tsp. garlic salt
1/4 tsp. pepper
1 deep-dish pie crust, baked
1-6 to 8 oz. pkg. sliced mozzarella cheese

Fry sausage and drain on paper towel. Sauté onion and green pepper in sausage grease for 3 to 4 minutes. Drain. Combine Cheddar cheese and flour in large bowl. Stir in cooked sausage, green pepper and onion. In another bowl, mix eggs, milk and seasonings. Mix well. Put half of sausage mixture into baked pie shell. Layer half of mozzarella cheese slices. Cover with remaining sausage mixture. Pour egg-milk mixture over all of this. Bake on cookie sheet in 350° oven for 20 minutes. Take out and place remaining mozzarella cheese on top. Bake for 10 more minutes.

Love is when two people say to each other with their eyes,
"With me you don't have to be on your guard."

EASY QUICHE

1/2 lb. bacon
1/4 lb. Swiss cheese
3 eggs, beaten
2 C. milk

1 tsp. salt
1/16 tsp. pepper
1 unbaked pie crust

Fry bacon until crisp; drain and crumble into pie crust. Shred cheese; arrange over bacon. Beat eggs slightly with beater. Add milk and seasonings and blend well. Pour over bacon and cheese. Bake in 400° oven for 30 to 40 minutes. Remove from oven while center appears soft. Cool for 5 minutes before serving.

PERFECT OMELET

6 eggs, divided
5 tsp. cornstarch
1 C. milk
1/2 tsp. salt
Pepper to taste
1 tsp. baking powder
Dash paprika

Chopped ham, cheese, onion, mushrooms, green peppers, sausage pre-fried and crumbled, bacon crumbled, or any other ingredient you would like to add. Add any of these ingredients in any combination you like.

Beat egg yolks; add cornstarch that has been dissolved in a little milk. Add the rest of the milk and salt. In a separate bowl, beat egg whites until stiff. Then add baking powder to egg whites. Blend everything together. Add any of the other ingredients you choose. Mix well. Pour into a hot skillet that has melted butter in it. Bake 20 to 30 minutes in 375° oven.

BAKED EGGS IN CREAM

6 eggs
1/2 tsp. salt

Paprika
6 T. cream

Break eggs into individual buttered ramekin. Cover eggs with tablespoon cream. Place in pan of hot water; set in moderate oven. Bake slowly about 10 minutes. Serve with hot buttered toast. Grated cheese may be added.

Goodness is the only investment that never fails.

EGGS A LA BENEDICT

8 eggs
4 English muffins

Hollandaise sauce
Paprika

Toast circular pieces of bread. Fry thin slice of boiled ham; put on top of toast. Fry slice of tomato, dredged with little flour, in pan that ham has been cooked in. Put cooked tomato on ham, then poached egg. Over all pour Hollandaise sauce.

HOLLANDAISE SAUCE

1/2 C. butter
1 T. flour
2 egg yolks
Juice of 1/2 lemon

Salt
1 C. boiling water
Few grains red pepper
Paprika

Cream butter and flour; add eggs one at a time. Add boiling water. Cook in double boiler until mixture thickens. Add salt and lemon juice.

POACHED EGGS

Pepper

Paprika

Boil water vigorously. Drop 1 egg from saucer into boiling water; lower heat. With spoon, dip boiling water over egg. Cover pan for 2 minutes. Remove egg to hot plate; add butter, salt and pepper.

SHIRRED EGGS

2 eggs
Salt
Pepper

1 tsp. cream
Paprika

Butter individual ramekin cups; cover bottom and sides with buttered cracker crumbs. Drop in eggs, little salt, black pepper, and cream. Set in pan with little hot water. Bake in moderate oven. Add paprika.

FOAMY OMELET

4 eggs	4 T. cream
1/2 tsp. salt	2 T. butter, melted
Pepper	

Beat yolks until creamy; add seasoning and cream. Beat whites of eggs until stiff. Cut and fold into egg mixture. Put butter in frying pan; pour in omelet and cook slowly. When set and slightly brown, place in broiler to dry top. Fold and serve immediately. Garnish with parsley and currant jelly.

The recipe for a good speech
includes some shortening.

You'll eat my stew... or else!

LeRoy's Beef Stew

2 lbs. lean beef stew meat
1 to 3 T. flour
1 to 2 T. vegetable oil
4 medium carrots, cut into
    1-inch slices
2 to 3 C. diced peeled potatoes
1 large onion, chopped
1 can (28 ounces) crushed
    tomatoes, undrained
2 C. boiling water
1 T. Worcestershire sauce
2 tsp. garlic powder
1 tsp. salt
1/2 tsp. pepper

In a large resealable plastic bag, combine the beef and flour; shake to coat. In a skillet, brown beef in batches in oil. With a slotted spoon, transfer meat to a 5-quart slow cooker. Add the remaining ingredients; stir. Cover and cook on low for 8 to 10 hours or until the meat and vegetables are tender.

LeRoy
Dorotik,
1942

LeRoy, 2000

Soups, Salads & Sandwiches

COUNTRY OVEN NEW ENGLAND CLAM CHOWDER

1 C. celery, diced
1 C. onion, diced
1/2 C. green pepper, diced
1/3 C. bacon fat or vegetable
  shortening
2 C. clam broth
2 large white potatoes, cubed
1/4 C. flour

1 C. water
2 C. half and half or milk
1 C. fresh clams, drained and chopped,
  or 2 cans chopped clams, drained
1 hard-cooked egg, chopped
Fresh parsley, chopped
Salt and pepper to taste

Sauté celery, onions and green pepper in bacon fat until transparent. Add clam broth and potatoes to pan; bring mixture to boil. Reduce heat; continue cooking until potatoes are barely soft. Whisk flour and water together until smooth. Stir into chowder and gently boil 5 minutes (to cook the flour). Reduce heat to medium. Add half and half, clams, egg, parsley and seasonings. Do not allow mixture to boil once half and half has been added. Heat thoroughly and serve.

HAMBURGER SOUP

1 lb. hamburger, browned
1/4 C. rice
2 large onions
1/4 C. celery
5 large potatoes, cubed

1 tsp. Worcestershire sauce
1 1/2 tsp. salt
1-14 1/2 oz. can beef broth
1-46 oz. can tomato juice
1-10 oz. box frozen mixed vegetables

Cook hamburger. Add all of the rest of ingredients, ending with the box of mixed vegetables on the top. I make this in a slow cooker; put the setting on #3 and cook about 6 hours with the lid on.

FRENCH CABBAGE SOUP

1/2 medium head cabbage
1 large potato
1 large onion

2 1/2 to 3 C. milk
3 T. butter
Salt and pepper to taste

Shred new green cabbage. Cut onion and potato into thin slices. Cook all three in heavy iron or aluminum saucepan over very low heat in very small amount of water (6 to 8 tablespoons). Keep tightly covered, stirring once or twice to prevent scorching. Cook until tender enough to mash with potato masher. After it is thoroughly mashed to a pulp, add milk, butter, salt and pepper. Heat until hot but do not boil. Serve with grated cheese on top.

GUMBO

1-1 lb. can stewed tomatoes
1/2 C. chopped green peppers
1 sliced onion
1 clove garlic

1/2 tsp. basil, crushed
1/4 tsp. pepper
3 drops hot pepper sauce
1 lb. okra (approximately), sliced

Combine all ingredients except okra and boil about 10 minutes. When done, add okra and cook until okra is tender. Salt to taste. This makes shrimp gumbo by just adding 1 pound frozen shrimp at the same time the okra is added.

NAVY BEAN SOUP

2 lbs. small navy beans
4 qts. hot water
1 1/2 lbs. smoked ham hocks

1 onion
Butter
Salt and pepper

Take 2 pounds of small navy beans; wash and run through hot water until beans are white. Put on stove with 4 quarts of hot water. Add 1 1/2 pounds of smoked ham hocks. Boil slowly about 3 hours in covered pot. After 2 1/2 hours, put 1 chopped onion in soup. When done, season with butter, salt and pepper.

POTATO SOUP

6 potatoes, cubed
2 carrots, sliced
2 celery stems, sliced
2 onions, diced
1 T. parsley, chopped

Salt and pepper to taste
5 C. water
4 chicken bouillon cubes
1-13 oz. can evaporated milk
1/3 C. margarine

Combine all ingredients except milk and margarine. Cover and cook over medium heat for 40 minutes. Add milk and margarine; simmer for 30 more minutes on low heat.

It's thinking about the load that makes one tired.

ROASTED CHICKEN NOODLE SOUP

2 tsp. olive oil
1 C. onion, chopped
1 C. carrots, diced
1 C. celery, sliced
1 garlic clove, minced
1/4 C. all-purpose flour
1/2 tsp. dried oregano
1/4 tsp. dried thyme

1/4 tsp. poultry seasoning
6 C. low-salt chicken broth
4 C. unpeeled baking potato, diced
1 tsp. salt
2 C. leftover roasted chicken, diced
1 C. evaporated milk
2 C. (4 oz.) uncooked wide egg
   noodles

Heat olive oil in a Dutch oven over medium heat. Add chopped onion, carrots, celery, and garlic clove; sauté 5 minutes. Sprinkle flour, oregano, thyme, and poultry seasoning over vegetables and cook 1 minute. Stir in broth, potato and salt. Bring to a boil; reduce heat and simmer, partially covered, 25 minutes or until potato is tender. Add roasted chicken, milk, and noodles and cook 10 minutes or until noodles are tender.

SOUP AND SANDWICH IN ONE

ON A SLICE OF TOAST PUT:
Fried ham or bacon slices
Sliced hard-boiled eggs

Sliced tomatoes

Cover with condensed mushroom soup. Top with grated Cheddar cheese; top with a dash of paprika. Put in oven at 350° to melt cheese.

SPLIT PEA SOUP

1 lb. split peas
1/4 lb. bacon ends
1 carrot
2 stalks celery

1/4 tsp. pepper
2 qts. water
Salt to taste
Medium onion

Cook all ingredients together until peas are mushy. Place soup in blender and blend until smooth.

SAUSAGE SOUP

1/2 link smoked pork and beef
   sausage, sliced with skin
3 Irish potatoes, chopped fine
1 bunch fresh onions or 1 large
   Bermuda onion, chopped fine

1 bunch celery tops, equaling about
   1 C., chopped
2 T. bacon drippings
1/4 C. yellow cornmeal
Salt and pepper to taste
Chili powder, optional

Boil in sufficient water until done, adding the cornmeal when soup is about half done to prevent scorching. This is a hearty soup to serve on a cold winter night.

SQUASH SOUP

1 lb. chopped squash
1 chopped onion
1 1/2 C. chicken broth

1/2 C. sour cream, optional
Salt and white pepper to taste
Dill

Boil squash, white pepper and onion in 1 cup chicken broth for 30 minutes. Purée in blender. Add 1/2 cup chicken stock and 1/2 cup sour cream. Chill 4 hours. Can be enjoyed warm or cold.

BEEF VEGETABLE SOUP

1 lb. hamburger
1/2 C. chopped onion
1 pkg. Hamburger Helper mix (beef
   noodle)
5 C. water

1 bay leaf
1/4 tsp. salt
1/8 tsp. pepper
1-16 oz. can whole tomatoes
1-10 oz. pkg. frozen mixed vegetables

Brown ground beef and onion; drain. Stir in sauce mix, water, bay leaf, salt, pepper and tomatoes. Heat to boiling, stirring constantly. Reduce heat; cover and simmer 10 minutes. Stir in noodles and vegetables. Cover and cook 10 minutes.

A "Leading Authority" is anyone
who has guessed right more than once.

VEGETABLE SOUP

1 lb. ground beef
2-1 lb. cans tomatoes
1-15 oz. can tomato sauce
1 C. water
1 can beef broth

1-20 oz. pkg. frozen soup mix or 2 cans
 Veg-All, drained
1 env. onion soup mix
2 tsp. sugar
 Salt to taste

Brown meat and drain off fat. Add remaining ingredients to meat. Simmer 30 minutes to 1 hour.

HEARTY VEGETABLE SOUP

2 lbs. stew beef, cut
1 C. chopped onion
1 tsp. minced garlic
2 T. olive oil
1/2 tsp. salt
1/2 tsp. pepper
3 cans beef broth

3 C. water
1 1/2 tsp. Italian seasoning
1 lb. can stewed tomatoes, drained
1 1/2 C. thinly sliced carrots
2 small zucchini, sliced
1 lb. can white corn, undrained
1 C. shell macaroni

Cut beef and onion into bite-sized pieces and brown with garlic in olive oil. Add salt and pepper. Add broth, water and seasoning and simmer for 1 hour. Add tomatoes, olives, liquid, carrots, zucchini, corn and macaroni and simmer 45 minutes.

BLACK-EYED PEAS SALAD

1 C. cooked ham, cut in cubes
5 C. cooked black-eyed peas
1 C. celery, chopped
1 green pepper, chopped

1 onion, chopped
2 tsp. prepared mustard
1 C. salad dressing
Salt and pepper to taste

Combine all ingredients. Put in refrigerator before serving.

*Two ways to become rich –
acquire great wealth or require few needs.*

BROCCOLI SALAD

1 C. mayonnaise
1/2 C. white sugar
2 T. lemon juice
1/2 diced onion

1 lb. bacon
12 oz. grated Parmesan cheese
1 bunch (2 stalks) broccoli

Combine mayonnaise, sugar and lemon juice. Mix well. Fry bacon until crisp; drain and break into small pieces. Wash and drain broccoli and break or cut into small flowerets. Pour mixture and onions over broccoli. Mix well and refrigerate. Right before serving, add bacon and cheese and mix again.

CABBAGE SLAW

1/2 C. sugar
1/2 C. vinegar
1/2 C. salad oil
1/4 tsp. salt

1/8 tsp. garlic powder
1/4 C. chopped bell pepper
3 qts. shredded cabbage
1/4 tsp. pepper

Combine sugar, vinegar, salt, garlic powder, and oil. Shake well to dissolve sugar. Pour over cabbage. Toss to coat. This dressing may be stored in refrigerator for several days in a cooled jar.

CHICKEN SALAD IN AVOCADO SHELLS

2 C. finely chopped white meat
   chicken
1/2 C. chopped celery
2 T. lemon juice
1/2 tsp. salt and pepper or to taste

Tabasco to taste
2 large avocados
2 hard-cooked chopped eggs
1/2 C. mayonnaise

Combine chicken, celery and mayonnaise. Stir in lemon juice and season with salt and pepper and Tabasco. Cut avocados in half; remove pits and scoop out pulp. Cut pulp into 1/2" pieces; dice and stir gently into chicken mixture. Fill avocado shells with mixture and sprinkle each serving with eggs. Serve on bed of lettuce.

CORN BREAD SALAD

1 recipe corn bread or 1 pkg. corn bread mix, baked, cooled and crumbled
10 or 12 slices bacon, cooked and crumbled
1 C. finely chopped celery
2 fresh green onions (some green tops), sliced very thin
2 large tomatoes, chopped fine
1/4 C. green pepper, finely chopped
2 T. chopped pimento, optional
2 hard-boiled eggs, chopped, optional

Mix all the preceding with enough mayonnaise to hold together. Chill at least 2 or 3 hours or overnight before serving.

CORN AND BUTTER BEAN SALAD

2 C. canned or frozen butter beans
1 C. white shoepeg corn
1 chopped green pepper
3 chopped spring onions
1/2 C. mayonnaise
Salt and pepper

Cook butter beans and corn (if frozen), until not completely done. Drain. Combine corn, butter beans, pepper, onions, seasoning and mayonnaise. Chill several hours.

CHINESE SALAD

1 can green beans
1 can wax beans
1 can Chinese mixed vegetables
1 can water chestnuts
1 C. chopped onion
ADD:
1/3 C. oil
2/3 C. wine vinegar
1/2 C. sugar
1 tsp. seasoned salt
1 tsp. pepper

Drain all vegetables and put in a large jar. Marinate 4 days, turning each day.

Anger never lacks for a reason,
but it's seldom a good one.

33

CRANBERRY SALAD

1 lb. frozen cranberries, ground
1 1/4 C. sugar
1 lb. small marshmallows

1 can crushed pineapple, drained
1/2 C. nuts
1 carton Cool Whip

Fold all ingredients together and freeze.

CUCUMBER SALAD

Beat 1/2 cup of thick cream to good consistency; add 1/4 teaspoon salt, a pinch of black pepper, and 2 tablespoons vinegar. Add 2 cucumbers, peeled and sliced. Sprinkle paprika over coated mixture.

ENGLISH PEA SALAD

DRAIN AND COMBINE:
1 lb. can small English peas, drained
1/2 C. onions, chopped
2 T. pimento, chopped

1 C. American cheese, grated
2 eggs, hard-boiled, chopped
3 slices bacon, fried, crumbled

IN SMALL BOWL, COMBINE:
3 to 4 T. mayonnaise
1/4 tsp. salt
1/2 tsp. sugar
1/2 tsp. Accent

2 tsp. lemon juice
Pinch garlic salt
1/4 tsp. pepper

Fold into pea mixture. Cover and chill at least 24 hours.

ENGLISH PEA SALAD

2-16 1/2 oz. cans English peas,
  drained
1/2 C. chopped celery
1/2 C. chopped sweet pickle

1-2 1/4 oz. jar green olives, sliced
3 hard-cooked eggs
1 C. mayonnaise
Paprika

Mix all ingredients except peas; then pour over peas and toss lightly. Sprinkle with paprika. Chill and serve.

FRENCH DRESSING

1/2 C. ketchup
1/2 C. sugar
1/2 C. olive oil
1/2 C. vinegar

Juice of 1 lemon
1 grated onion
1 tsp. paprika

Blend ingredients together and chill until ready to use.

FROZEN FRUIT SALAD

2 T. cherry juice
1 T. lemon juice
1/2 C. canned apricots, diced
1/2 C. pineapple, drained and diced
  (flat can)
1/2 C. grapes, halved

1/2 C. cherries, drained and chopped
  (large jar)
1/4 C. sugar
1/4 C. mayonnaise
1/2 C. whipping cream

Add cherry and lemon juice to fruits and sugar. Whip cream until fluffy. Add mayonnaise and fold into fruit mixture. Pour in mold and cover to freeze.

FROZEN FRUIT SALAD

1-8 oz. pkg. cream cheese
3/4 C. sugar
1-10 oz. pkg. frozen strawberries,
  undrained

1-20 oz. can crushed pineapple,
  drained
2 sliced bananas
1/2 C. chopped nuts
2-1.5 oz. pkgs. Dream Whip

Blend cheese and sugar. Add fruit and nuts. Whip Dream Whip and fold into cheese and fruit mixture. Freeze.

GARDEN SALAD

1 head cauliflower
1 head broccoli
1 pkg. radishes
1 green pepper
2 cucumbers

1 onion
2 pkgs. tri-colored spiral noodles
2 jars ranch dressing
1 pkg. shredded Cheddar cheese

Dice vegetables into bite-size pieces. Cook noodles; drain and cool. Combine all ingredients in big bowl and add dressing; stir. Chill before serving.

GERMAN POTATO SALAD

2 lbs. (4 to 5) potatoes
4 T. oil
4 T. vinegar
2 tsp. salt

1/4 C. bouillon or chicken broth (if homemade stock not available, use 1/4 C. water with chicken bouillon cube)
1 tsp. finely minced onion
Dash pepper
4 slices well-done bacon

Boil unpeeled potatoes until tender. Dilute warm bouillon or chicken broth with vinegar, onion, salt and pepper. Peel and thinly slice potatoes while they are still warm. Pour the diluted ingredients over potatoes; then add oil. Crumble bacon over mixture. May be served warm or cold.

LIME JELLO SALAD

2-3 oz. pkgs. lime jello
1/4 C. pineapple juice
3 1/2 C. water
2 C. miniature marshmallows

1 large carton fine cottage cheese
2 pkgs. Dream Whip or whipping cream
1 C. (8 oz. can) crushed pineapple
1 C. chopped pecans, optional

Dissolve jello in boiling water. Add pineapple juice. Chill until partially firm, then whip. Add marshmallows, cottage cheese, drained pineapple and pecans. Fold in whipped topping or cream. Chill overnight.

MACARONI AND CHEESE AND BACON SALAD

2-7 1/4 oz. pkgs. Kraft macaroni and cheese
1 lb. bacon, fried crisp

1 C. chopped pickles
1 1/4 C. mayonnaise

Cook macaroni and cheese mix according to package directions. Cool. Crumble crisply fried bacon and mix rest of ingredients with macaroni and cheese. Serve when chilled.

Don't waste fresh tears over old griefs.

MACARONI SALAD

16 oz. macaroni
1 green pepper, chopped
1/2 onion, chopped
1 cucumber, sliced
Celery and carrots, optional

DRESSING:
1 C. mayonnaise
1/4 C. vinegar
8 oz. evaporated milk

Cook, drain and cool macaroni. Add vegetables. Mix dressing until well blended. Pour over macaroni and vegetables; mix well. Chill and serve.

MACARONI SALAD

1 lb. curly macaroni, cooked
3 carrots, shredded
2 C. shredded cheese
1 onion, chopped
1 C. diced celery
1 1/2 C. diced ham

1 can Eagle Brand milk
1 C. sugar
3/4 C. vinegar
1 pt. mayonnaise
Salt and pepper to taste

Combine, chill and serve.

MACARONI SALAD

1 pkg. short cut elbow macaroni,
  cooked according to pkg. directions
  (do not rinse)
1 C. celery, chopped
1 C. green onions, chopped
1 C. sweet gherkin pickles, chopped
1 C. mayonnaise

1 tsp. salt
1/2 tsp. black pepper
1/4 tsp. white pepper
1 T. mustard seed
1/4 C. pickle juice
2 tomatoes
Paprika

Add celery, green onions, and pickles to macaroni. Combine mayonnaise, salt, peppers, and mustard seed; add to first mixture. Then stir in pickle juice. Cut up tomatoes and add to salad. Chill; garnish with paprika and serve.

The mind is like a parachute –
it only works if it's open.

PICKLED BEET SALAD

1-1 lb. can sliced beets
1/2 C. vinegar
2 T. sugar
1/2 tsp. salt

3 or 4 small cloves
1 small bay leaf
1 small onion, sliced

Drain beet liquid into saucepan, reserving beets, and add vinegar, sugar, salt, cloves, bay leaf and onion. Bring to the boiling point. Reduce heat and simmer 5 minutes. Add beets and refrigerate overnight.

SALAD:
1-3 oz. pkg. lemon gelatin
3/4 tsp. salt
1 C. boiling water
3/4 C. drained pickle beet liquid
1 tsp. prepared horseradish

2 tsp. grated onion
Dash of pepper
3/4 C. drained, diced pickled beets
3/4 C. diced celery

Dissolve gelatin and salt in boiling water. Add beet juice, horseradish, onion and pepper. Chill until very thick (egg white consistency). Fold in beets and celery. Pour into 1-quart mold or 5 individual molds. Chill until set.

PEA SALAD

2 cans peas, drained
1 C. chopped celery
1 C. cubed cheese

3 hard-boiled eggs
1/2 C. Miracle Whip

Mix all together.

ROQUEFORT DRESSING

1 C. buttermilk
2 C. mayonnaise
2 T. Worcestershire sauce

2 tsp. garlic salt
4 oz. blue cheese
1 1/2 oz. Roquefort cheese

Blend all ingredients thoroughly; chill.

SLAW

Cabbage
Red onions
Green peppers
1/2 C. salad oil

1/2 C. sugar
1/2 C. vinegar
Salt and pepper

Slice cabbage in thin strips. Chop red onion and green pepper. Mix oil, sugar, and vinegar and pour mixture over the vegetables. Marinate 6 hours, stirring often. Add salt and pepper to taste.

SEVEN LAYER VEGETABLE SALAD

Iceberg lettuce
6 hard-cooked eggs
2 small onion or bunch of spring
   onions, chopped
1-10 oz. pkg. frozen peas, thawed

1-8 oz. pkg. Swiss cheese, grated
1 C. mayonnaise
4 to 5 pieces of bacon, fried and
   crumbled
Salt to taste

Tear lettuce and cover bottom of 11x13" casserole. Then layer other ingredients. Ice with mayonnaise and crumble bacon on top. Chill several hours.

SOUR CREAM POTATO SALAD

2 T. grated onion
2 T. chopped parsley
2 T. dill pickles
2 T. pimento
2 T. vinegar
1 T. prepared mustard

1 tsp. salt
1/2 tsp. fresh ground pepper
1 C. sour cream
4 C. diced cooked potatoes
1 C. chopped celery
3 hard-boiled eggs, chopped

Combine all ingredients. Toss until well blended.

The best thing about telling the truth –
you don't have to remember what you said.

SPAGHETTI SALAD

Spaghetti noodles
1/2 C. mushrooms
1/2 C. celery
Grated Cheddar cheese
Salad Supreme spices

Chopped tomatoes
1/2 C. onion
1/2 C. green pepper
Chopped green and black olives
Large bottle Zesty Italian dressing
Pepperoni

Cook spaghetti noodles, broken in small pieces. Drain and cool. Mix all ingredients except spices and dressing. Add 1 cup dressing 24 hours before serving. Stir, cover and put in refrigerator. The day of serving, add 1 cup of dressing and spices. Stir and serve.

SUMMER SAUERKRAUT SALAD

1-16 oz. can sauerkraut, drained
   and rinsed
1/2 C. red or green pepper, chopped
2 C. celery, chopped

1 small onion, chopped
1/2 C. sugar
1/4 tsp. salt
1/8 tsp. pepper

Combine all ingredients. Refrigerate until serving time.

SPANISH SALAD

1 head lettuce
1 can ranch style beans, rinsed
1 C. grated Cheddar cheese

1/2 onion
2 large tomatoes

Toss all together.

1 pkg. Fritos, crushed

1 bottle Kraft Catalina French dressing

Add Fritos last. Pour dressing over salad.

SPINACH SALAD

Fresh spinach
2 boiled eggs
1 C. sliced, fresh mushrooms
1/2 C. chopped green onions

1/2 C. sliced radishes
Tomato wedges
5 strips bacon
Oil and vinegar dressing

Wash and stem spinach. Clean all other vegetables and prepare for salad. Fry bacon and crumble. Toss all ingredients in salad bowl, except eggs and tomatoes. Slice eggs and wedge tomatoes. Arrange on top for looks. Pour oil and vinegar dressing on top of salad sparingly.

TACO SALAD

4 C. shredded lettuce
1/2 C. sliced green onions with tops
1 lb. ground chuck
1/4 C. chopped onions

1-15 oz. can chili beans or kidney
  beans, drained
1-4 oz. can taco sauce
8 oz. Cheddar cheese, shredded

Toss lettuce and green onions in large bowl. Refrigerate. Brown meat in skillet. Add chopped onion and cook until tender. Stir in beans and taco sauce. Simmer 15 minutes. Spread hot meat mixture over lettuce in bowl. Sprinkle with cheese. Serve without stirring or tossing.

TAPIOCA SALAD

4 C. water
Pinch of salt
1 box raspberry jello

1/2 C. baby pearl tapioca
1 carton frozen raspberries
1 carton Cool Whip

Boil tapioca and salt 10 minutes. Remove from heat. Add 1 package raspberry jello and 2/3 cup sugar. Add raspberries (frozen and defrosted). When ready to serve, stir in carton of Cool Whip. Strawberry jello and strawberries may be substituted.

The one you influence today
just might influence thousands in the future.

TUNA SALAD

1-9 oz. can chunk tuna
1 C. chopped celery
2 T. sweet pickle juice
1/2 C. finely chopped spring onions
   and greens

1/2 C. mayonnaise
1 T. mustard
3 chopped hard-boiled eggs
1/2 C. chopped sweet pickles

Combine the ingredients in a large mixing bowl. Cook and drain a 7 ounce package of salad noodles or spaghetti rings and stir in with salad. Salt and pepper to taste. Chill and serve on lettuce leaves. Sprinkle with paprika.

WATERGATE SALAD

1 large Cool Whip
1-16 or 20 oz. can crushed pineapple
1 small pkg. instant vanilla pudding

1/2 C. nuts, chopped
1/2 C. or more miniature marshmallows

Mix well. Mixture will thicken as it cools in refrigerator. Do not drain pineapple. Use dry pudding.

EGG SALAD SANDWICHES

12 boiled eggs, chopped
1/2 C. fresh parsley, chopped
4 green onions, chopped
1-4 oz. can chopped ripe olives
3 T. mayonnaise

1 tsp. mustard
Juice of 1 fresh lime
Salt and pepper to taste
Sliced black olives

Mix together. Serve on bread or toast.

CHICKEN SANDWICHES

1 C. finely chopped cooked chicken
Enough mayonnaise to moisten
   mixture
Little salt

Paprika
1/4 C. pimento olives, chopped fine
   OR 2 hard-boiled egg yolks, mashed
Celery salt

Spread on slices of bread. Lettuce may be used if desired. Sliced pickles may also be added.

BUTTERED CHEESE SANDWICHES

FOR EACH SANDWICH YOU WILL NEED:

2 slices bread	Mayonnaise or salad dressing
1 slice American cheese	Butter or margarine

Spread butter or margarine on each side of both slices of bread. Heat a square griddle to medium-high. Put both slices of bread on griddle. When brown, turn 1 slice; add cheese and mayonnaise. Top with brown side of other slice of bread. Turn and brown top of sandwich. Remove when brown.

Love is better than money and
friends are better than possessions.

Notes

He kills it...
cleans it and cooks it.

She kills it...
he still cleans it,
he still cooks it!

Main
Dishes,
Meat &
Wild Game

MUSHROOM STEAK

2 lbs. round steak, tenderized
1/4 C. flour
1/4 C. oil
1 large onion, chopped

1-4 oz. can mushrooms
1 can cream of mushroom soup
1/2 C. milk (mix milk and soup together)

Cut round steak into serving size pieces. Flour steak and brown in oil in an electric fry pan. Add onions and mushrooms. Pour soup mixture over all; cover. Simmer 1 hour.

SWISS STEAK

1/3 C. flour
1/2 tsp. salt
1/4 tsp. pepper
1 slab round steak

2 T. shortening
1-14 oz. can whole tomatoes
1/2 C. diced onion
Green pepper slices

Stir together first three ingredients. Sprinkle on both sides of meat and pound in. Cut into small pieces. Brown meat in shortening. Simmer covered for 1 hour. Add water as necessary. Add remaining ingredients and simmer covered for 30 minutes.

CHICKEN FRIED STEAK

1 lb. steak, cut in serving pieces
1 egg
2 T. milk

Salt and pepper
Flour

Season steak with salt and pepper. Roll in flour; dip in well-beaten egg to which the milk has been added. Then roll in flour again. Fry at once in hot shortening to a light brown.

BOWL WINNER'S BARBECUE BURGERS

1-4 to 6 lb. beef roast
1-10 3/4 oz. can cream of chicken or mushroom soup

1 1/4 C. barbecue sauce
1 env. Lipton dry onion soup mix

In roasting pan, cover meat with soup. Pour barbecue sauce over soup. Sprinkle dry soup mix over meat. Cover and bake roast in 350° oven for 3 hours or until tender enough to shred. Drain fat and remove any bones. Shred meat and serve on buns.

PATTY BAKE

Fry or grill several hamburger patties, seasoned the way you like them. It is best to use ground chuck. Place each cooked patty on a separate piece of foil large enough to wrap the patty. Put sliced potatoes, carrots, bell pepper and onion on top of patty. Sprinkle with salt, pepper, garlic salt and Accent. If you like you can put a jalapeno pepper that has been cut in half and seeded on top of this. Put ketchup and a dash of Worcestershire sauce over each patty. Close tightly and bake on cookie sheet at 350° for 1 hour.

GROUND BEEF BURGERS

1 lb. ground beef
1 chopped onion

1 C. green pepper

Fry until brown. Drain off the grease.

ADD:
1/2 C. ketchup
1 T. mustard
1 T. vinegar

1 T. brown sugar
1 T. flour
Salt and pepper

Simmer together. Serve on buns.

BEEF ROAST

3 to 5 lb. beef roast, any cut you
    prefer
2 to 4 C. beef broth
Minced onion
Garlic

GRAVY:
Beef broth from cooked roast
2 T. cornstarch mixed with 1/4 C.
    cold water

Preheat oven to 350°. Set beef roast in baking pan that has a lid. Pour beef broth in pan, at least to 3" deep. Sprinkle minced onion and a small amount of garlic into broth. Cover with lid. Bake at least 2 hours or more if larger cut.
GRAVY: Pour broth into saucepan. Heat to boiling. Add cornstarch mixed with cold water and stir constantly until thick. May need to add water if too thick, or more cornstarch and water mixture if not thick enough. Makes a rich beef flavored lump-free gravy.

BEER ROAST

1-4 lb. arm roast
1 C. ketchup
1 T. sugar, if desired
1 large onion, chopped

1/2 green pepper, chopped
Salt and pepper to taste
1 bottle beer

Sprinkle roast with salt and pepper; sprinkle with a little flour and brown in hot fat. Add sugar, onions, and green pepper. Cover with ketchup and pour beer around roast; cover. Bake at 350° F. for 2 hours and 30 minutes. Remove from pan; thicken liquid for gravy.

PEPSI ROAST

1-3 to 4 lb. beef roast
1 pkg. dry onion soup mix

1 can cream of mushroom soup
1-12 oz. can Pepsi Cola

Put roast in pan and top with dry onion soup mix. Spread the soup over the onion mixture and slowly pour the Pepsi over. Cover. Cook slowly in a 300° oven for 5 to 6 hours. Makes its own gravy! You may also do this in a slow cooker.

BEEF NOODLE CASSEROLE

1-8 oz. pkg. wide egg noodles
2 lbs. ground chuck
1/2 C. bell pepper, chopped
6 green onions, chopped
Salt to taste
1-15 oz. can tomatoes

1-6 oz. can tomato sauce
1/2 tsp. garlic powder
1-8 oz. pkg. cream cheese
1/2 C. sour cream
1/2 C. cottage cheese
1/2 C. Cheddar cheese

Cook and drain noodles according to package directions. Brown the ground chuck. Add bell pepper, onions, and salt to taste. Cook until tender. Add tomatoes, tomato sauce, garlic powder, cream cheese, sour cream, cooked noodles and cottage cheese. Place in a 3-quart casserole dish and top with Cheddar cheese. Bake 30 minutes at 350°.

A friend is one who knows you as you are,
understands where you've been,
accepts who you've become,
and still gently invites you to grow.

BEEF STROGANOFF

2 lb. round steak
1 can beef broth soup
1 can mushroom soup
1 small can mushrooms, drained

1 C. sour cream
1 small onion, diced
Worcestershire sauce

Cut steak into 1" squares; flour and brown in skillet along with diced onion. (The browner the meat the better.) Add the soups and mushrooms; simmer for 1 1/2 to 2 1/2 hours. The last hour add sour cream and Worcestershire sauce (2 to 3 dashes or to your taste). Serve over noodles.

BAKED CASSEROLE

SLICE IN BAKING DISH:
Potatoes
Carrots

Onions

ADD:
1 lb. browned beef or pork
1/3 C. uncooked rice
1 T. sugar

Salt and pepper to taste
2 1/2 C. tomato juice
1 C. peas

Bake 1 hour at 350° until potatoes and carrots are done.

TATER TOT CASSEROLE

2 lbs. ground meat
2 lb. pkg. frozen tater tots
1 can cream of mushroom soup

1 can cream of chicken soup
Salt and pepper to taste
1 small can evaporated milk

Place ground meat in bottom of casserole dish. Put tater tots on top of meat. Mix soups and milk; pour on top of potatoes. Season to taste. Bake at 350° for 45 minutes to 1 hour.

A faithful friend is a source of strength.
And he who finds such a friend has found a treasure.

PETE'S HASH

2 lbs. ground chuck or round
1 medium chopped onion
2 or 3 small zucchini squash, sliced
Salt and pepper to taste
2 tsp. chili powder

1/2 tsp. paprika
Dash Accent
2 cans Ro-Tel or 1 large can chopped
  tomatoes

In 1 tablespoon butter, sauté onions and zucchini until soft. Brown ground meat. Add zucchini and onions. Add rest of ingredients; mix well. Simmer on low heat 15 to 30 minutes.

MEAT LOAF

1 1/2 lb. ground beef
1 C. bread crumbs
1 egg, beaten
2 T. finely chopped onion

1 T. finely chopped green pepper
Salt and pepper to taste
1/2 can tomato sauce
1 tsp. Lea and Perrins sauce

Mix and pack into loaf pan. Bake at 375° about 1 1/2 hours, basting from time to time with following sauce.

SAUCE:
1/2 can tomato sauce
1/2 can water

3 T. brown sugar
1 T. vinegar
1 tsp. prepared mustard

Mix well with beater.

EASY MEAT LOAF

2 lbs. ground beef
2 eggs
Ketchup

Mustard
1 C. saltine crackers, crushed
Chopped onion

Crumble ground beef into large bowl; add eggs and mix. Add desired amount of ketchup and mustard; stir. Add crushed saltine crackers and chopped onion; mix all together. Press into 13x9x2" pan. Bake at 350° for 30 minutes; then drain excess grease. Pour ketchup all over the top and bake for 30 more minutes or until done.

BEANS AND CHILI

1 lb. pinto beans
1 lb. hamburger meat
1 small onion
1 small clove garlic, optional

1 can tomatoes
1 T. chili powder, or as desired
Salt and pepper to taste

Soak beans overnight. Put in saucepan and boil until tender. Fry the hamburger, onions, and garlic until done. Add to the beans with chili powder and tomatoes; let boil together for a few minutes.

CROCK POT SWISS STEAK

2 lb. round steak
1 env. beef mushroom soup mix
  (dry)

Carrots, sliced
Celery, sliced
Potatoes, sliced

Cover both sides of steak with dry soup mix. Place in crock pot. Add sliced carrots, potatoes and celery (desired amount). Cook on low for 6 to 8 hours.

CROCK POT BEEF STEW

Potatoes
Carrots
Mixed vegetables
1 small can whole kernel corn

Cubed roast or steak
1 can tomato sauce
Onion
Salt and pepper

Use desired amount of all ingredients and cook on low for 8 to 10 hours.

CAMP STEW

1 hen, cooked, boned and cut in
  bite-size pieces
2 1/2 lbs. round steak, cooked
  tender and cut in bite-size pieces
1 1/2 lbs. lean pork, cooked tender
  and cut in bite-size pieces

6 1/2 lbs. potatoes, peeled and cut in
  large pieces
2 1/2 lbs. sliced onion
2-16 oz. cans tomatoes
1-14 oz. bottle ketchup
Salt and pepper
1 stick butter or margarine

Combine chicken, steak, pork, potatoes, onions, tomatoes, ketchup, salt, pepper and butter and cook until vegetables are tender. Stir often to prevent sticking.

BEER STEW

4 onions, coarsely diced
4 T. butter
2 T. sugar
3 lbs. chuck stew meat, cut in
  bite-size cubes
2 T. olive oil
2 T. flour
2 C. beer

2 T. vinegar
1 C. beef stock
1 bunch celery, chopped
1 bunch carrots, sliced crosswise
3 sprigs parsley
1 bay leaf
Pinch thyme
Salt and pepper

Sauté onion in butter; add sugar to help brown. Sauté meat in olive oil; add flour. Combine onion, meat, beer, vinegar, beef stock and bring to a boil; add celery, carrots, herbs and spices and simmer 2 hours. Whole small potatoes may be added if desired. This may be doubled and frozen. Stew is always better the second day.

SWEET AND SOUR ORANGE CHICKEN WINGS

3 lbs. chicken wings
1 1/2 C. flour
1 1/2 T. baking powder
1 tsp. ground ginger
1/2 tsp. salt

1 C. water
1/2 C. vegetable oil
Vegetable oil for frying
Sweet and sour orange sauce

Combine flour, baking powder, ginger and salt. Stir in water and 1/2 cup oil. Using pastry brush, coat chicken pieces. Preheat oven to 250°. Pour oil into large deep heavy skillet or deep fat fryer to 2" deep. Heat to 350°. Fry chicken wings a few at a time. Remove to paper toweling. Garnish with green onion brushes, orange slices and sweet red pepper strips.
SWEET AND SOUR ORANGE SAUCE: Combine 1 1/2 cups orange juice, 1/4 cup cider vinegar, 1/4 cup soy sauce, 1/3 cup brown sugar, 1/2 teaspoon ground ginger and 1 clove garlic in medium saucepan. Combine 2 tablespoons cornstarch and 2 tablespoons dry sherry. Stir into saucepan; cook, stirring constantly until mixture thickens.

A true friend walks in when the rest of the world walks out.

GRILLED CHICKEN SKEWERS

1/2 lb. boneless, skinless chicken
  breasts, cut into thin strips
1/2 lb. bacon slices
1/3 C. lemon juice

1/3 C. honey
1 1/2 tsp. Lawry's lemon pepper
  seasoning
1/2 tsp. Lawry's seasoned salt

Thread chicken strips and bacon slices onto wooden skewers. In shallow dish, combine remaining ingredients. Add prepared skewers and refrigerate 1 hour or overnight. Grill or broil 10 to 15 minutes, basting with marinade, until chicken is cooked through and bacon is crisp. Makes 2 servings.
PRESENTATION: Garnish with lemon wedges. Serve as a light entrée or cut in half and serve as appetizers.
HINT: Soak wooden skewers in water before grilling to prevent them from burning.

CRISPY GOLDEN FRIED CHICKEN

1-2 to 3 lb. broiler-fryer chicken,
  cut up
1 T. salt
1 qt. cold water
1 1/2 C. all-purpose flour
1 T. paprika

2 tsp. salt
1 tsp. black pepper
2 eggs, beaten
2 T. milk
Salad or vegetable oil

Rinse chicken pieces in a mixture of 1 tablespoon salt and 1 quart water; drain chicken and chill 1 hour, if time permits. Combine flour, paprika, salt and pepper in a brown paper bag. Place chicken in egg and milk mixture and let stand while oil heats to 350° to 375°. Place chicken pieces in sack and shake vigorously, holding top securely. Cook chicken in deep fat until done. Drain well on paper towels and paper bags.

BARBECUED CHICKEN

10 chicken halves

SAUCE:
1 large jar Durkee's Sauce
6 lemons, sliced
1 C. vinegar
2 sticks oleo

2 T. dry mustard
2 T. sugar
2 T. salt

Cook chicken on grill for 10 minutes on each side. Meanwhile, mix Durkee's Sauce, lemons, vinegar, oleo, mustard, sugar and salt. Cook until oleo melts, then start basting chicken with sauce. Cook 1 1/2 to 2 hours, very slowly.

OVEN BARBECUED CHICKEN

3/4 C. vinegar
1 tsp. paprika
1 tsp. mustard
2 T. ketchup

1/2 stick butter
1 tsp. salt
2 T. Worcestershire sauce
1 cut up chicken

Combine first seven ingredients and bring to a boil in saucepan. Pour over chicken. Bake, basting frequently, at 350° for 1 hour.

BARBECUE SAUCE

1/4 C. vinegar
1/2 C. water
2 T. sugar
1/2 tsp. salt
1/4 tsp. cayenne pepper

1 thick slice lemon
1 sliced peeled onion
1/4 C. butter
1/2 C. ketchup
2 T. Worcestershire

Mix everything except ketchup and Worcestershire in saucepan and simmer 20 minutes, uncovered. Add ketchup and Worcestershire sauce; bring to a boil. Makes about 1 3/4 cups.

BARBECUE SAUCE

1/2 C. vinegar
1 1/2 C. water
1/4 C. brown sugar
Pepper and salt to taste
1/4 C. Worcestershire sauce
4 tsp. prepared mustard

1 T. lemon juice
1 small onion, chopped
1/2 C. margarine
1 C. ketchup
1/4 tsp. garlic powder

Combine vinegar, water, sugar, mustard, pepper, garlic powder, lemon, onion and margarine. Simmer mixture for about 20 minutes. Add ketchup and Worcestershire sauce. Stir and remove from heat.

RITZ CRACKER CHICKEN

1 sleeve Ritz crackers, crushed
1/3 C. Parmesan cheese

1/4 C. butter, melted
4 to 6 boneless chicken breasts

Mix crushed crackers and Parmesan cheese. Cover chicken with cracker-cheese mixture and place in lightly greased baking dish. Drizzle with melted butter. Bake at 350° for 45 minutes to 1 hour. Do not cover.

EASY CHICKEN

Coat 5 pounds chicken parts with a mixture of 1/2 cup flour, 1 teaspoon paprika, and 1/2 teaspoon salt. Put mixture in a paper sack and add about 4 pieces chicken at a time and shake until thoroughly coated. Place in single layer (skin-side down) in 2-13x9x2" pans. Dribble 1/4 cup melted butter over chicken. Bake in hot oven at 400° F. for 20 minutes. Turn chicken; bake 20 minutes longer. Stir 3 cans mushroom soup and 1 can water until smooth. Pour over chicken. Reduce heat to 350° and bake 45 minutes to 1 hour more.

EASY CHICKEN AND RICE

1 chicken, cut up
1 C. uncooked rice
1 env. dry onion soup mix

1 can cream of celery soup
1 can cream of chicken soup
1 can water

Mix rice, soup and water in baking dish. Add raw chicken pieces and sprinkle with dry soup mix. Cover and bake at 350° for 2 hours.

CHICKEN BAKE

1 cut up chicken or pieces of
  choice, with or without skin
1 can chicken broth
1 sliced lemon with rind
2 to 4 cloves garlic

Chopped onions to taste
1 sprig fresh rosemary or ground,
  to taste
Salt and pepper to taste

Line glass baking dish with chicken pieces. (Glass is important, size of dish dependent on amount of chicken.) Pour broth over chicken. Add remaining ingredients. Bake in 325° oven until chicken pulls away from bone, 2 to 4 hours. VARIATIONS: Omit lemon and rosemary. Use soy sauce, ginger and chopped green pepper to taste; or sun dried tomatoes, jalapeno peppers and sliced black olives.

KING RANCH CHICKEN

1 large chicken, cooked, deboned,
  and cubed
1 pkg. (12) corn tortillas
1 can cream of chicken soup
1 can cream of mushroom soup

1 can Ro-Tel tomatoes
1 C. onion, chopped
1 C. green peppers, chopped
1/2 C. celery, chopped
1 1/2 C. grated Cheddar cheese

Sauté onion, green pepper, and celery in 1/4 cup butter. Soften tortillas in chicken broth; break into pieces and line 11x13" pan. Layer chicken, sautéed mixture and the soups and tomatoes. Top with cheese. Bake at 350° for 30 minutes.

CHICKEN SPAGHETTI CASSEROLE

1-5 lb. chicken, cook until tender and dice
1 pkg. spaghetti, cooked in chicken stock (if necessary add more water)

10 carrots, cooked in water until done
2 onions, chopped
Few stalks of celery, chopped
2 green peppers, chopped

Place in a large baking dish that has been rubbed with garlic. Add 1 small can mushrooms, 1-No. 2 can tomatoes or tomato soup, the chopped chicken, carrots, spaghetti, all the chicken stock (may have to add a little water so it won't get too dry). Add salt and pepper to taste. Mix all ingredients well and bake for 1 hour at 350°. Remove from oven; sprinkle top with 1 pound grated Wisconsin cheese.

CHICKEN SPAGHETTI

5 lb. chicken
2 boxes spaghetti or 1-3 lb. pkg.
1-No. 2 can tomatoes
1 C. ripe olives, cut in half
1 can cream of mushroom soup

1 lb. American cheese
1 large onion
1 bell pepper
1 T. parsley
1 T. celery salt
Salt and pepper to taste

Cook chicken, then cook spaghetti in chicken broth. Sauté onion and bell pepper in butter until nearly done. Add mushroom soup. Dice chicken and add spaghetti, onion mixture, cheese and tomatoes. Bake in casserole at 350° for 45 minutes, stirring occasionally.

CHICKEN SPAGHETTI

Cook 1 chicken and deboned. Cook 1 pound spaghetti in broth. Add water if necessary. Drain.

MIX:
1 can Cheddar cheese soup
1 can cream of mushroom soup

1 can Ro-Tel tomatoes and chilies
The cut up chicken

Mix with spaghetti in a 2-quart casserole. Top with Velveeta cheese. Bake 30 minutes at 350°.

CHEESE ENCHILADAS

1 1/2 lbs. marble Jack cheese,
  shredded
1 medium onion, diced
3 large eggs

1/4 C. cooking oil
12 corn tortillas
1-10 oz. can black olives, sliced
2-10 oz. cans enchilada sauce

Preheat oven to 325°. Stir together 2/3 of the cheese with 1/2 of the diced onion. Stir in the eggs until thoroughly mixed, and set aside. Pour the oil into a heavy frying pan over medium heat. Fry tortillas one at a time in oil until soft, turning once, about 5 to 10 seconds on a side. While each tortilla is still soft, spoon cheese mixture into center and roll up. Place rolled tortillas in a 9x13" baking dish and cover with remaining cheese, onion, and olives. Pour enchilada sauce over all and bake, uncovered, for 30 to 35 minutes.

CHICKEN ENCHILADA CASSEROLE

1 C. chopped onion
1/2 C. chopped green bell pepper
2 T. butter or margarine
2 C. chopped, cooked chicken or
  turkey
1-4 oz. can green chili peppers,
  rinsed, seeded and chopped
3 T. butter or margarine

1/4 C. all-purpose flour
1 tsp. ground coriander seed
1/2 3/4 tsp. salt
2 1/2 C. chicken broth
1 C. sour cream
1 1/2 C. shredded Monterey Jack
  cheese (6 oz.)
12-6" tortillas

In large saucepan, cook onion and green pepper in the 2 tablespoons butter or margarine until tender. Combine in a bowl with chopped chicken and green chili peppers; set aside. In same saucepan, melt the 3 tablespoons butter or margarine. Blend in flour, coriander and salt. Stir in chicken broth all at once; cook and stir until thickened and bubbly. Remove from heat; stir in sour cream and 1/2 cup of cheese. Stir 1/2 cup of the sauce into the chicken. Dip each tortilla into remaining hot sauce to soften; fill each with about 1/4 cup of the chicken mixture. Roll up. Arrange rolls in a 13x9x2" baking dish; pour remaining sauce over. Sprinkle with remaining cheese. Bake, uncovered, in 350° oven about 25 minutes or until bubbly.

The secret of contentment is know how
to enjoy what you have.

GREEN CHILI CASSEROLE

1 1/2 lbs. ground beef
1 chopped onion
1 can cream of mushroom soup
1 can cream of chicken soup
1 small can evaporated milk

1 can green chilies
1 lb. grated cheese (American or Cheddar)
1 pkg. flour tortillas (10 to 12), torn into pieces

Brown ground beef and onion. Add soups, milk and green chilies. Spray a 2-quart casserole with cooking spray. Layer as follows: 1/2 meat mixture, 1/2 tortillas, 1/2 cheese. Repeat. Bake at 350° for 30 minutes.

GREEN ENCHILADAS

1 can cream of chicken soup
1 small can evaporated milk
1/2 lb. Velveeta cheese
1 small can green chilies, chopped

1 small jar pimentos
1 dozen flour tortillas
1/2 lb. longhorn cheese, grated
1 C. chopped onions
1 lb. ground beef, lightly browned

Heat soup, milk and Velveeta cheese in double boiler until cheese is melted. Add chopped chilies and pimentos. Combine grated longhorn cheese, onions and meat. Soften tortillas in hot grease. Fill each tortilla with meat mixture; roll tightly and place in long baking dish. Pour cheese sauce over tortillas. Cover with aluminum foil. Bake at 350° for 30 minutes.

MEXICALI CHICKEN AND CHEESE BAKE

3 C. cooked, cubed chicken
8 oz. shredded Jack cheese
12 oz. can corn, drained
10 3/4 oz. can cream of chicken soup
1 C. flour
1/4 C. cornmeal
1 3/4 tsp. baking powder

1/2 tsp. chili powder
1 1/2 C. milk
1/2 C. melted margarine
3 eggs, beaten
4 oz. chopped green chilies, drained
2 oz. jar pimento, chopped and drained

Preheat oven to 350°. Grease 9x13" pan. Combine chicken, 1 cup cheese, corn and soup; blend well. Spoon into greased casserole pan. Combine flour, cornmeal, baking powder and chili powder. Add milk, margarine and eggs. Stir until dry ingredients are moistened. Batter may appear lumpy. Stir in chilies and pimento. Pour over chicken mixture. Bake for 50 to 60 minutes or until golden brown and set. Sprinkle remaining cheese over top and return to oven until cheese melts. Let stand for 10 minutes (very important). Garnish with sour cream and/or salsa.

SANTA FE CASSEROLE BAKE

1 lb. lean ground beef
1-1.25 oz. pkg. Lawry's taco spices and seasonings
2 C. chicken broth
1/4 C. all-purpose flour
1 C. sour cream

1-7 oz. can diced green chilies
1-11 oz. pkg. tortilla chips
2 C. (8 oz.) grated Monterey Jack or Cheddar cheese
1/2 C. sliced green onions, including tops

In medium skillet, brown ground beef, stirring, until cooked through; drain fat. Add taco spices and seasonings; blend well. In small bowl, combine broth and flour. Add to meat mixture; bring to a boil to slightly thicken. Stir in sour cream and green chilies. In lightly greased 13x9x2" baking dish, place half of chips. Top with half of beef mixture, half of sauce, half of cheese and half of onions. Layer again with remaining ingredients, ending with onions. Bake in 375° F. oven for 20 to 25 minutes or until cheese is melted. Let stand 5 minutes before cutting. For additional flavor, top with guacamole.

STUFFED PEPPERS WITH BEEF

4 large green peppers
3/4 lb. ground chuck
1/2 chopped medium onion
1 T. Chili-O seasoning mix
1 T. Worcestershire sauce

Dash of Tabasco
1 tsp. celery salt
1-14 oz. can tomatoes
Pepperidge Farm dressing
Grated Parmesan cheese

Scoop out inside of peppers and boil cases 5 minutes. Drain and set aside. Brown beef in skillet and push to one side. Lightly brown onion and mix with beef. Add other ingredients except dressing and cheese. When mixed, add only enough Pepperidge Farm dressing to make a moist mixture. Stuff mixture in pepper cases and set upright in custard cups or muffin pans. Top with Parmesan cheese. Bake at 325° until hot.

The smallest good deed is better than the greatest intention.

TAMALE PIE

CRUST:

1 C. Masa Harina	1 T. salad oil
1/2 tsp. salt	1 C. water

Combine all ingredients in bowl; mix well. Press into a greased 9" pie plate. Set aside.

FILLING:

2 T. butter or margarine	1-7 oz. can whole kernel corn, drained
1/2 C. chopped onion	1/2 C. chopped ripe olives
1/3 C. chopped green pepper	2 tsp. chili powder
1 clove garlic, crushed	1 tsp. salt
1 lb. ground beef	2 T. flour
1-10 oz. can tomatoes, drained	1/2 C. grated Monterey Jack cheese

Melt butter in large saucepan. Sauté onion, green pepper and garlic until tender. Add meat and brown. Drain fat; add remaining ingredients except cheese. Pour into crust. Bake at 400° F. for 20 to 25 minutes. Remove from oven; sprinkle with cheese. Return to oven for 5 minutes.

BUBBLE PIZZA

2 pkgs. Pillsbury biscuits	1 pkg. Canadian bacon
2 lbs. ground beef, browned	1/2 pkg. pepperoni
1 can pizza sauce	1 green pepper, chopped
1/2 C. onion, chopped	1-12 oz. pkg. mozzarella cheese
1 can mushrooms	

Cut Pillsbury biscuits in quarters. Mix in ground beef, sauce, onions, mushrooms, Canadian bacon, pepperoni and green peppers. Put in greased cake pan. Bake at 350° for 1/2 to 1 hour or when biscuits are brown. Put mozzarella cheese on top and bake until done.

Age is mostly a matter of mind.
If you don't mind, it doesn't matter.

ITALIAN BAKE

1 lb. ground beef, browned
1 small onion
1-15 oz. can tomatoes
1 C. macaroni, cooked and drained
1/2 C. water

1/2 tsp. each oregano, basil and
   garlic salt
1/4 tsp. pepper
1/2 C. Cheddar cheese
1/2 C. mozzarella cheese

Mix first seven ingredients together and put into casserole. Top with the two cheeses. You may add any of the following ingredients: pepperoni, mushrooms, green pepper or olives. Bake at 375° for 20 minutes.

LASAGNA

MEAT SAUCE:
1 lb. lean ground beef
1 clove garlic, minced
1 tsp. basil
1 tsp. salt
1-6 oz. can tomato paste
1 big can stewed tomatoes

CHEESE FILLING:
1 egg
1 C. cottage cheese
1/2 C. ricotta cheese
1/4 C. Parmesan cheese
1 T. parsley flakes
1/2 tsp. salt
1/4 tsp. pepper

CHEESE FILLING: Beat egg; stir in remaining ingredients.
MEAT SAUCE: Brown meat slowly over medium heat; drain fat. Add remaining sauce ingredients and simmer, uncovered, for 20 to 30 minutes, stirring frequently. Cook lasagna noodles in large pan of boiling water until tender; drain and rinse with cold water. Layer noodles, cheese mixture and meat sauce in casserole pan. Top with grated Parmesan cheese and grated mozzarella cheese. Bake at 350° for 45 minutes or until hot and cheese is bubbly.

Keep your words soft and sweet;
you never know when you may have to eat them.

SPAGHETTI AND MEAT BALLS

1 lb. ground beef
1/2 C. fine dry bread crumbs
1/4 C. grated American cheese
1 T. chopped parsley
2 cloves garlic, minced

1/4 C. milk
2 beaten eggs
Salt and pepper to taste
1-8 oz. pkg. long spaghetti

Mix all ingredients together except spaghetti, and mix very well. Roll into balls the size of a golf ball. Brown in a small amount of oil and add the balls to the sauce and simmer.
SAUCE: Brown 1 medium onion, chopped, in 2 tablespoons oil.

ADD:
2 1/2 C. canned tomatoes
1-8 oz. can tomato sauce
2 C. water
1 tsp. salt

1/2 tsp. pepper
1 T. sugar
1 clove garlic, minced
2 bay leaves

Bring to a boil; then lower heat to simmer 2 or 3 hours. Prepare your spaghetti according to directions on package and serve with sauce and meatballs.

TUNA CASSEROLE

1 can tuna
3 C. cooked macaroni
1/2 C. chopped pimento

1/2 C. chopped celery
1 small chopped onion
1 can cream of chicken soup
Cheese

Mix first six ingredients together in large mixing bowl and then put in casserole dish and top with cheese. Bake at 350° for 30 minutes.

WIENERS AND RICE

2 T. bacon drippings
1 medium onion, chopped
8 frankfurters, sliced in 3/4" pieces

3/4 C. canned tomatoes
1 C. boiling water
1 C. uncooked rice

Melt drippings in a large heavy skillet. Add onion and cook until lightly browned and tender. Add franks and brown slightly. Add remaining ingredients. Mix well and cook, stirring occasionally, for 30 minutes or until rice is tender.

SKILLET SUPPER

1 lb. beef smoked sausage	2 1/2 C. beef bouillon
1 large onion, sliced	1-10 oz. pkg. frozen green peas
1 1/2 C. uncooked rice	1-4 oz. can mushrooms, pieces and
2 T. butter or margarine	stems

Cut sausage into six pieces. Cook onions and rice in butter until onions are limp. Stir in bouillon, peas and mushrooms. Bring to a boil; stir and place sausage on top. Cover tightly; reduce heat to simmer. Cook 15 minutes until rice is tender and liquid is absorbed.

BAKED TURKEY

Wash a 10 to 14 pound turkey and remove giblets and neck. Salt and pepper inside and out. Brush inside and out with melted butter. Stuff bird with dressing. Place breast side down and bake at 450° for 30 minutes. (A rack placed in a broiling pan works well.) Turn turkey breast side up and reduce temperature to 325° for about 4 to 4 1/2 hours. If turkey browns too quickly, make a tent of aluminum foil to place on top of turkey. The quick hot temperature seals the juice in the breast so that it does not dry out.

CORN BREAD TURKEY DRESSING

6 biscuits	3 1/2 C. turkey stock
1 pan corn bread	Salt to taste
2 slices bread	1/2 C. onion
1 T. parsley	1/2 C. celery
1 tsp. poultry seasoning	1/3 C. butter
Dash pepper	2 eggs

Crumble and mix together first three ingredients. There should be about 6 cups of crumbs. Add seasonings and turkey stock. Sauté onion and celery about 5 minutes in butter. Add to dressing. Beat the eggs slightly and combine all ingredients. Mix well. Bake in a greased casserole uncovered, at 350° for 1 hour. (Can stuff the turkey with part of the dressing.)

We wouldn't worry so much about what other people think of us
if we knew how seldom they actually did.

BARBECUED HAM

3 lbs. ham, sliced thin

BRING TO BOIL:

1 C. ketchup
1 3/4 C. water
6 T. brown sugar

2 T. Worcestershire sauce
1/4 C. vinegar
2 T. finely chopped onion

Simmer all ingredients (except ham) for 20 minutes. Thicken with 1 tablespoon cornstarch mixed with 1 to 2 tablespoon water. Put all of the ham and sauce together in crock pot; mix well. Cook all day or all night.

PORK BARBECUE

3 1/2 to 4 lb. pork shoulder roast, boned and skinned
1/2 T. salt
Pepper to taste

1/4 C. water
1 T. sugar
3/4 C. vinegar

Place meat in slow cooker. Mix all the ingredients and pour over roast. Cook on high for 1 hour. Then cook for 12 hours on low. After meat is cooked, chop up while still in slow cooker. Serve from cooker. Save juice for reheating. Makes 20 to 25 barbecue sandwiches.

PORK CHOPS 'N POTATO BAKE

6 pork chops
Vegetable oil
Seasoned salt
1-10 3/4 oz. can cream of
  mushroom soup

1/2 C. milk
1/2 C. sour cream
1/4 tsp. pepper
Shredded potatoes
4 oz. shredded Cheddar cheese

Brown chops in lightly greased pan. Sprinkle with seasoned salt and set aside. Combine soup, milk, sour cream, pepper and 1/2 teaspoon seasoned salt. Stir in potatoes and 1/2 cup cheese. Spoon mixture into 9x13" baking pan. Arrange pork chops over top of potatoes. Bake, uncovered, at 350° for 40 minutes. Then top with remaining cheese and bake, uncovered, for 5 minutes.

OVEN BARBECUED SPARERIBS

3 to 4 lbs. pork ribs
1/4 C. chopped onion
1/2 C. water
2 T. vinegar
1 T. Worcestershire sauce

1/4 C. lemon juice
2 T. brown sugar
1 C. chili sauce
1/2 tsp. salt
1/4 tsp. paprika

Combine all ingredients except pork ribs; simmer for 20 minutes. Set aside. Place ribs in pan and cover with aluminum foil. Bake for 15 minutes at 450° F. Reduce heat to 350° F. and continue baking 45 minutes or until tender. Pour sauce over meat and return to oven for 5 minutes longer.

BASTING SAUCE FOR GRILLED PORK CHOPS

2 T. butter
1/2 C. soy sauce
1 lemon
1/2 tsp. onion salt

Freshly ground pepper, generous dash
1/4 tsp. Tabasco or to taste
Bourbon or sherry to taste, optional

In small saucepan, mix butter, soy sauce, lemon (cut in half, squeeze juice in and drop shells in), onion salt, pepper, Tabasco and bourbon or sherry. Boil 5 minutes. Baste pork chops often the last half hour of cooking on grill, keeping sauce hot, if possible. Enough for 4-1" chops.

SPANISH PORK CHOPS

4 to 6 center-cut pork chops, 1/2"
   thick
Vegetable or salad oil
1 tsp. salt
1/2 tsp. chili powder
1/2 tsp. pepper

1/2 C. chopped onion
1/3 C. bell pepper
1/2 C. long grain rice
1-28 oz. can tomatoes
1 C. grated Cheddar cheese

Brown pork chops in oil in skillet. Drain and sprinkle with mixture of salt, chili powder and pepper. Top with onion, bell pepper and rice. Pour tomatoes over all. Simmer 1 hour. Add cheese and simmer until it melts.

BAKED BASS

1-5 lb. bass (or equivalent)
1 large chopped onion
1 chopped green pepper
1/2 stick margarine
2-8 oz. cans tomato sauce
1 can whole tomatoes
Juice of 1 lemon

1 C. cooking wine
1/2 C. green onions
Parsley
Dash Tabasco sauce
Salt, pepper, garlic powder to taste
Lemon slices

Sprinkle fish with lemon juice and season generously ahead of time, preferably overnight. Sauté lightly onions and bell peppers in margarine. Add tomato sauce and whole tomatoes and cook over medium heat for 45 minutes in uncovered pot. Add 2 cups water and seasoning to taste, adding dash of Tabasco sauce. Cook for 25 minutes over medium heat. Add wine and pour mixture over fish and bake in 325° oven for 40 minutes. Baste several times. Sprinkle parsley and onion tops over and serve with slices of lemon for garnishment.

BEER BATTER FRIED FISH

1 C. Bisquick
1 egg

1/2 C. beer
1/2 tsp. salt

Mix batter well. Dip fish in flour first, then in batter. Fry in heated oil. Makes 2 pounds of fish.

DEEP SOUTH HUSH PUPPIES

2 C. cornmeal
3/4 C. milk
1/2 C. water

2 tsp. baking powder
1 tsp. salt
2 onions, chopped fine

Add water and milk to sifted dry ingredients. Add chopped onions. Work dough until you can mold hush puppies about the size of an English walnut. (You may need more cornmeal.) The original southern hush puppies were oblong cakes. Fry in deep fat or oil about 370° until a beautiful brown color. These are usually served with fish, so when possible fry in skillet after fish is removed.

BAKED FISH WITH TOMATO SAUCE

2 C. tomatoes
1/4 C. water
1 slice onion
3 T. flour
3/4 tsp. salt

Pepper
1 T. butter
2 lbs. white fish, clean carefully
Onion powder

Cook ingredients until thick, stirring constantly. Place fish in greased baking pan. Pour sauce over fish. Bake about 40 minutes, basting often. Serve immediately. Sprinkle with paprika and celery salt if desired.

FISH FILLET SUPREME

2 or 3 lbs. fish fillets (catfish, bass, trout, or salt water fish)
1 stick butter (not margarine)
Juice of 1 lemon, large to medium size
1/8 tsp. onion powder or 1 T. finely chopped green onion tops

1 tsp. salt (1/2 tsp. for salt water fish)
1/8 tsp. pepper
1 T. Worcestershire sauce
1 tsp. paprika
1 T. Parmesan cheese

Place butter in shallow baking dish or broiling pan bottom. Put into 400° to 450° oven until butter is browned but not burned. This is what makes the fish so good. Place fillets, fleshy side down, in hot butter and return to oven for 10 to 15 minutes. Then turn fillet over and baste with butter and juice. Sprinkle each fillet with lemon juice, Worcestershire, cheese, salt, pepper, onion powder, and paprika. Place in oven for about 5 to 6 minutes or until done. Place under broiler and broil quickly. Baste fillets with sauce.

A well-adjusted person is one
who makes the same mistake without getting nervous.

OYSTER PIE

1 pt. fresh oysters and liquor	1 C. evaporated milk
1 T. butter	1/4 C. canned green peas
1/2 C. chopped celery	1-2 oz. jar chopped pimento
1 medium chopped onion	Salt and pepper to taste
1/2 lb. sliced fresh mushrooms	Dash paprika
4 T. butter	1-9" pastry crust
2 T. flour	

Stew oysters and liquor until edges of oyster curl. Set aside. Melt 1 tablespoon butter. Add celery and onion and cook until tender; add mushrooms and cook covered about 8 more minutes. Set aside. Melt 4 tablespoons butter. Add flour and brown lightly. Add milk, stirring until thick. Thin with 1 to 2 tablespoons oyster liquor. Add sautéed vegetables, oysters (drain remaining liquor), peas, pimento, salt, pepper and paprika. Combine well. Pour into greased casserole. Top with pastry; dot with butter and bake in 350° oven 10 to 15 minutes to brown pie crust.

BARBECUED SHRIMP

1/2 tsp. salt	3 T. chopped parsley
1/2 tsp. garlic powder	2 tsp. onion powder
1/2 C. salad oil	1/2 tsp. pepper
1/4 C. soy sauce	2 lbs. large shrimp, peeled, uncooked
1/4 C. lemon juice	

Combine salt, garlic, oil, soy sauce, lemon juice, parsley, onion and pepper to make marinade, mixing well. Place shrimp in shallow dish and cover with marinade. Refrigerate about 3 hours. Put shrimp on shish kabob skewers. Grill over fire for 4 minutes per side. May broil in oven.

Character is not made in a crisis – it is only exhibited.

SHRIMP CREOLE

3 T. cooking oil
2 T. flour
1 clove garlic
1-1 lb. can tomatoes
1-8 oz. can tomato sauce
1 1/2 tsp. salt
1 tsp. sugar

1/2 tsp. chili powder
1 T. Worcestershire sauce
Dash Tabasco sauce
1 green bell pepper, chopped
1 medium onion, chopped
2 lbs. shrimp

Cook shrimp by boiling in shrimp and crab boil; peel and clean. Mix together the oil, flour, garlic, tomatoes, tomato sauce, salt, sugar, chili powder, Worcestershire sauce, Tabasco, bell pepper and onion. Cook uncovered in Dutch oven over low heat for 1 to 1 1/2 hours. Add shrimp to the mixture at the last 20 minutes of cooking time. Serve over rice.

SCALLOP PRIMAVERA

1-10 oz. can cream of onion soup
1-10 oz. soup can milk
1 large lemon
1 medium onion, diced
4 T. butter
1 C. mushrooms, sliced

2 C. broccoli, diced
8 oz. scallops, thawed if frozen
1/4 C. flour
Lemon-pepper
1 lb. pkg. angel hair pasta

Prepare soup with milk per the instructions on the can. After the soup is smooth, squeeze 1/2 of the lemon into the soup; stir and remove from heat. In a large frying pan, sauté the onion in the butter until onion is translucent. Add mushrooms, broccoli, and scallops; continue to sauté until scallops are cooked, 3 to 5 minutes. Stir in flour and juice from remaining 1/2 of lemon, until flour is well dissolved. Pour the soup over the scallop and broccoli; stir until it thickens. Serve with angel hair pasta.

SMOTHERED LIVER AND ONIONS

1 lb. liver, sliced
Salt and pepper to taste
3 T. fat

1 large onion, chopped
Flour

Salt and pepper liver and roll in flour. Brown on both sides in hot fat. Add onion and enough water to cover. Simmer until done, adding more water if needed.

LEG 'O LAMB

Season lamb with salt and pepper and slivers of garlic, if desired. Put 1/3 cup red wine vinegar, 2/3 cup oil, 1/4 teaspoon dry mustard and 1 clove garlic together and stir. Pour over seasoned lamb and bake. Baste lamb every 15 to 30 minutes. Bake in 325° oven until meat thermometer reads 180°. Quartered onions may be baked with this.

IRISH STEW

2 1/2 lb. boneless lamb stew meat
4 medium onions, sliced
1 T. chopped parsley
1 T. fresh thyme or 1 1/2 tsp. dried
   thyme leaves

1 1/2 tsp. salt
1/4 tsp. pepper
6 medium potatoes, peeled and halved
   or quartered
6 medium carrots, cut in strips

Arrange half of lamb in heavy kettle or Dutch oven. Layer onions on meat; layer remaining meat and sprinkle on part of seasonings. Arrange potatoes and carrots on top. Sprinkle on rest of seasonings. Add 1 1/2 cups water or enough to cover meat but not potatoes. Bring to boil; reduce heat and simmer 2 1/2 hours or until meat is tender. Serve in bowls.

OVEN BARBECUED VENISON, LAMB OR GOAT

3 lbs. venison, lamb or goat

Sear the meat; place in roasting pan.

BARBECUE SAUCE:
1 C. ketchup
2 T. Worcestershire sauce
1/4 C. vinegar
1 T. butter
1/2 lemon, quartered

1 T. salt
1/8 tsp. cinnamon
1/8 tsp. allspice
1 onion, chopped

Mix in saucepan and bring to a boil, stirring to avoid burning. Simmer 10 minutes. Cover seared meat with sauce and roast in moderate oven at 350° for 1 1/2 to 2 hours. Turn and baste every 30 minutes.

VENISON CHILI

2 lbs. coarsely ground venison
1 T. bacon drippings
2 T. chili powder
1 tsp. sage
1/2 tsp. pepper
1 tsp. salt
1 tsp. cumin

1 C. chopped onion
2 cloves garlic
2-15 oz. cans Spanish style tomato
  sauce
2 C. water
1-23 oz. can chili beans

Brown venison in bacon drippings; add chili powder, sage, pepper, salt, cumin, onions and garlic. Stir in tomato sauce, water and beans and simmer for 1 hour.

VENISON MEXICAN CASSEROLE

1 lb. ground venison
1-10 1/2 oz. can each of cream of
  mushroom soup, cream of
  chicken soup, and Cheddar
  cheese soup

1-10 oz. can tomatoes and green chilies
Salt to taste
12 tortillas
1 C. grated Cheddar cheese

Brown meat in skillet; add soups, chopped tomatoes and chilies and salt. Stir well. In greased 9x13" baking dish, layer 6 tortillas. Spread half of meat mixture over tortillas. Repeat. Top with grated cheese. Cover and bake 25 to 30 minutes at 350° F.

VENISON CHEESEBURGER PATTIES

2 lbs. ground venison and pork
1 lb. mild diced Cheddar cheese

1 T. chopped onion
Salt and pepper

Mix and allow to "cure" briefly in refrigerator or form into patties and freeze until ready for use. Fry in Teflon skillet on low heat; cover with lid during cooking.

VENISON CHILI

2 pounds ground venison, browned in 1/2 cup hot bacon drippings. Season with salt and pepper. Add 1 medium onion, chopped fine, 3 tablespoons chili powder, and 3 tablespoons flour. Sear a little longer. Add 1 cup tomato sauce and enough water to cover. Simmer about 1 hour. Garlic may be added.

VENISON JERKY

Cut 1 pound venison in 1/4" slices.

COMBINE THE FOLLOWING INGREDIENTS:

1 tsp. salt	1/2 tsp. onion powder
1/4 tsp. pepper	1/4 tsp. Worcestershire sauce
1/4 tsp. garlic powder	1 drop Tabasco sauce

Marinate meat in mixture overnight. Hang over oven rack (will not drip) at 150° F. for 3 hours.

SMOKED VENISON OR JERKY MEAT

Cut choice cuts of tenderloin or hindquarter of deer into 2" or 3" strips, any length. Place meat in large bowl; cover with hot water for about 10 minutes. Drain and sprinkle with Tender Quick meat cure, using 1 ounce per pound of meat. Cover and store in refrigerator or cool place for 2 or 3 days. Pepper may also be added at this time. Smoke in a covered pit for 8or 10 hours with very low heat, using either oak, hickory or mesquite wood for coals. Do not overheat or meat will be too dry.

VENISON MEAT LOAF

1 1/2 lbs. venison and 1/2 lb. pork, ground together	4 to 6 slices dry bread soaked in water
Salt and pepper to taste	1-15 oz. can tomatoes or 8 oz. can tomato sauce
1/2 chopped green pepper	2 eggs
1 chopped onion	

Heat meat in bacon drippings until it has changed color; remove from heat. Then add green pepper, onions, bread, tomatoes or sauce and then the 2 eggs, slightly beaten. Mix and turn into 1 large loaf pan or 2 small loaf pans and bake 45 minutes at 325° F.

The difference between flattery and a compliment is sincerity.

VENISON PAN SAUSAGE

8 lbs. venison
4 lbs. fresh pork
1/2 C. salt

2 T. black pepper
1 tsp. red pepper
Little brown sugar

Add seasoning to meat; grind together and form into 1 pound rolls. Wrap and freeze. Slice as needed.

VENISON ROAST

Season roast with salt and pepper. Cut slits and insert pieces of onion. Brown in 1/2 cup shortening and place in roaster with strips of bacon across top. Bake at 350° F. for 1 hour. Pour 1/2 cup hot water over meat. Bake another hour, basting frequently. A can of tomatoes added to juice of roast improves flavor. Potatoes and carrots may be added.

VENISON SAUSAGE

To every 20 pounds of meat (2/3 venison and 1/3 pork), add 1 cup (8 ounces) butcher salt, 1/3 cup coarse ground black pepper and 2 teaspoons saltpeter. Mix salt, pepper and saltpeter together. Sprinkle over meat. Grind and stuff in casings. Smoke for 2 or 3 days. May be frozen fresh or dried. Meat proportion may be 1/2 venison and 1/2 pork.

VENISON STEAK

Cut steak 3/4" to 1" thick. Put garlic salt and pepper on it. Let set for 10 minutes. Flour well and fry slowly in shortening.

VENISON STEAK

2 lbs. venison steak
1/2 C. vinegar
1 C. water

1 tsp. salt
1/2 tsp. black pepper
1 C. self-rising flour

Cut venison into serving pieces; soak in vinegar and water for 3 to 4 hours. Drain. Roll steaks in mixture of salt, pepper and flour. Brown on both sides in hot shortening.

VENISON OR LAMB STEW

2 lbs. venison, cut in small pieces
1 tsp. salt
1/4 tsp. chili powder
1/8 tsp. black pepper
2-8 oz. cans tomato sauce
2 C. water

2 T. flour
4 carrots, cut up
1 medium onion, chopped
1 C. peas, canned or frozen
4 potatoes cooked with 1/2 tsp. salt
    and mashed

Roll meat in flour, salt, pepper and chili powder mixture. Brown in 2 tablespoons shortening. Add tomato sauce and water. Simmer for 1 1/4 hours. Add vegetables and simmer another 1/2 hour. Pour into buttered 9x13" casserole. Place mashed potatoes around inside of rim. Bake at 375° F. for 15 minutes or until potatoes are light brown.

VENISON STROGANOFF

1 pkg. Lipton onion soup
1 can whole mushrooms

2 round steaks, cut in cubes, beat
    and peppered
2 small cartons sour cream

Brown meat in butter or oil; stir in onion soup, mushrooms and sufficient water to cover. Simmer about 1 hour. Stir in cream just before serving. Serve over noodles. (No salt is needed on meat as the seasoning in soup is sufficient.)

CHARCOALED DOVE

1 C. prepared mustard
1 stick (1/2 C.) butter
1 T. brown sugar
Dash Tabasco

Dash Worcestershire sauce
Dash black pepper
20 doves

Place first six ingredients in a double boiler and melt together. Stir until smooth. Grill doves slowly over low coals, basting often, for 30 to 40 minutes.

COUNTRY STYLE DOVES

6 to 8 doves
1/2 C. flour
Salt and pepper to taste

1/2 C. oil
2 T. flour
1 C. water

Shake doves in bag with 1/2 cup flour, salt and pepper. Fry in oil until crisp. Remove from pan. Make a gravy using 2 tablespoons drippings and 2 tablespoons flour. Blend well and add water. Stir. Add doves and simmer 20 to 30 minutes. (May need to add more water as it simmers.) Serve with rice. Double recipe if you have more doves.

BAKED DOVES

8 to 10 doves
1/2 stick margarine
1/2 C. celery, chopped
1/2 C. onion, chopped
Salt

Pepper
2 cubes chicken bouillon
1 C. boiling water
White wine, optional

Salt and pepper doves. Brown in melted margarine on all sides. Place in casserole dish and cover with celery and onions. Dissolve bouillon cubes in water and pour over doves. Cover and place in 325° oven. Bake 1 hour 15 minutes. A little white wine may be added the last 15 minutes, but it isn't necessary.

SOUTHERN FRIED QUAIL

Dry, pick quail. Clean and wash thoroughly. Salt and pepper and dredge with flour. Have a deep, heavy frying pan with close-fitting lid half full of hot fat. Put in quail. Cook for a few minutes over a hot fire; then cover skillet and reduce heat. Cook slowly until tender, turning the quail to the other side when golden brown. Serve on hot platter garnished with slices of lemon and sprigs of parsley.

When you see a light at the end of the tunnel,
it means there's a train headed your way.

BAKED QUAIL

12 quail
1 C. flour
1/2 tsp. salt
1/4 tsp. pepper
1/2 C. (1 stick) melted butter

1 tsp. thyme
1-10 3/4 oz. can cream of mushroom
  soup
1 C. white wine

Dredge quail in mixture of flour, salt and pepper. Brown in butter. Arrange in 9x13" Pyrex baking dish. Sprinkle with thyme. Mix soup and wine. Pour over birds. Cook covered for 4 hours at 250°. May be frozen after cooking. Serve with brown or wild rice.

FRIED RATTLESNAKE

Secure a rattlesnake. Carefully kill the snake and remove head. Avoid the fangs at all costs. Bury head at least 1 foot deep. Now you skin the snake. Remove intestines and wash. Cut into 3" pieces. To 2 or 3 cups of flour, add 1 tablespoon chili powder, 1 teaspoon paprika, 1/2 tsp. garlic powder, 1 teaspoon salt, 1 teaspoon onion powder, 1/2 teaspoon celery salt, and 1/2 teaspoon Accent and 1 teaspoon black pepper. Dredge damp pieces of snake in flour mixture and fry in deep fryer until done. This is also a good flour mixture for fried chicken.

CHILDREN LEARN WHAT THEY LIVE

If a child lives with criticism, he learns to condemn.
If a child lives with hostility, he learns to fight.
If a child lives with ridicule, he learns to be shy.
If a child lives with shame, he learns to feel guilty.
If a child lives with tolerance, he learns to have patience.
If a child lives with encouragement, he learns to have confidence.
If a child lives with praise, he learns to appreciate.
If a child lives with fairness, he learns about justice.
If a child lives with security, he learns to have faith.
If a child lives with approval, he learns to like himself.
If a child lives with acceptance and friendship, he learns to find love in the world.

Notes

No, Grandma, please don't cook...

we like
it much
better
when
you
let Grandpa cook!

Vegetables

ASPARAGUS PEA CASSEROLE

1-10 oz. pkg. asparagus
2 hard-cooked eggs, sliced
1 pkg. frozen peas
6 slices American cheese, sliced
   diagonally
1 can cream of mushroom soup

1/4 C. sour cream
1/4 tsp. onion powder
1/4 tsp. white pepper
2 T. butter or margarine
1/4 C. dry bread crumbs

Cut asparagus into 2" pieces. Layer peas and asparagus in lightly greased 8" square dish. Top with eggs and half of cheese. Combine soup, sour cream, onion, and pepper. Spoon half over cheese. Layer rest of asparagus and peas and spoon rest of soup mixture on top. Melt butter; add bread crumbs. Sprinkle over mixture. Microwave on high 8 minutes. Cover; let stand 5 minutes.

BAKED FRESH ASPARAGUS

2 lbs. fresh asparagus
2 T. minced fresh parsley
2 T. olive oil

2 T. melted butter (no substitute)
Salt and pepper

Wash, peel and break off ends of asparagus. Arrange in a single layer in a buttered oblong baking dish. Sprinkle with parsley, salt and pepper. Drizzle olive oil and butter over asparagus. Cover tightly and bake at 400° for 20 to 25 minutes.

BAKED BEANS

1 small onion
1/2 lb. hamburger
1/2 lb. bacon, chopped
1/4 C. brown sugar
1/4 C. sugar

1/4 C. ketchup
1/2 tsp. dry mustard
1 can kidney beans
1 can pork and beans
1 can butter beans

Brown onion, hamburger, and bacon. Add remaining ingredients. Put in large casserole and bake at 350° for 1 to 1 1/2 hours, depending on thickness of beans desired.

BAKED BEANS

3 lb. can pork and beans
1 1/2 C. brown sugar
3 T. ketchup
3 T. barbecue sauce, any kind

1 T. or more mustard
1 large onion, diced
1-4 oz. can mushrooms, diced
1 lb. bacon, optional

Put all ingredients in a crock pot and mix together. Put on low heat for 8 hours; refrigerate for 8 hours or more. Do this up to three times because it seems to get better each time you cook the beans. The beans are ready to enjoy after the third cooking.

BLACK BEANS

1 lb. dried black beans
1 large green pepper, chopped
2 large onions, chopped
4 to 6 cloves garlic, chopped
1/2 C. olive oil
6 C. water

1/4 lb. fat back, cut into 2" cubes
3 bay leaves
1/3 C. vinegar
1 1/4 tsp. salt
1/2 tsp. ground pepper

Wash beans. Sauté green pepper, onions and garlic in olive oil until tender. Bring 6 cups water to a boil and add all ingredients. Turn heat to low and cook covered 3 to 5 hours until beans are tender. Serve over rice with chopped raw onions as garnish.

CHEESY BROCCOLI BAKE

1 1/2 lbs. fresh broccoli or 2 pkgs.
   frozen broccoli
2 eggs
1 can cream of mushroom soup
1 C. milk

1 C. chopped onions
1/2 C. chopped celery
1-10 oz. pkg. grated Cheddar cheese
Buttered bread crumbs

Cook broccoli until tender. Drain well and put into 2-quart casserole. Mix together soup, milk, eggs, onion, celery and grated cheese. Pour over broccoli. Put buttered bread crumbs on top. Bake at 350° for about 45 minutes.

BROCCOLI CASSEROLE

1 stick margarine
2 C. quick rice
Diced onion
2 C. water

1 bag frozen broccoli cuts, chopped fine
2 C. Velveeta cheese, cubed, OR 1-8 oz.
  jar Cheez Whiz
1 can cream of mushroom soup

Combine margarine, rice and onion in 2-quart casserole dish and microwave on medium heat for 2 1/2 minutes. Stir and microwave on medium for another 2 to 2 1/2 minutes. Add water. Let set for 5 to 7 minutes or until most of the water is absorbed. Cook broccoli until 2/3 done. Then add broccoli to the rice mixture. Next add the cheese and cream of mushroom soup. Bake at 350° for 20 to 30 minutes until hot and bubbly.

CHEESE CABBAGE CASSEROLE

1 head of cabbage
2 T. oil
2 T. flour

1 C. milk
1 C. Velveeta cheese
Ritz crackers

Chop cabbage and boil until tender; drain. Meanwhile, heat oil and add flour and milk to make a white sauce. Add cheese and stir until melted. Layer in large baking dish with one layer crackers, a layer of cabbage and a layer of cheese sauce. Keep layering and top with crackers. Bake at 350° for 30 minutes. Can use soda crackers instead of Ritz.

CORN PUDDING

1-10 oz. pkg. frozen corn
1 stick melted butter
3 T. sugar
2 T. flour

2 beaten eggs
1/2 C. milk
Salt to taste

Thaw corn. Mix remaining ingredients together. Combine with corn in buttered 1 1/2-quart casserole dish. Bake uncovered at 350° for 45 minutes until set and golden brown on top.

CORN MOUSAKA

17 oz. can corn, drained (can use
   frozen)
1 1/2 lbs. hamburger
1 T. flour
1-8 oz. can tomato sauce
1/2 tsp. garlic salt

2 eggs, beaten
1 1/2 C. cottage cheese
1/2 lb. mozzarella cheese
1/4 C. Parmesan cheese
1 can mushrooms
Onions, optional

Put corn in bottom of 1 1/2- to 2-quart casserole. Brown hamburger; add flour and cook. Add tomato sauce, garlic salt, onion and mushrooms. Pour over corn; bake 15 minutes at 350°. Combine eggs, cottage cheese and mozzarella cheese and pour over meat. Top with Parmesan cheese. Bake at least 20 minutes. Let stand at least 15 minutes before serving.

SCALLOPED CORN

1 can cream-style corn
1 can whole kernel corn
1 chopped onion

1 chopped green pepper
3 eggs
1 C. sour cream
1-25¢ size corn muffin Jiffy mix

Mix all ingredients together and put in a greased 9x13" pan. Bake for 45 minutes at 325°.

SCALLOPED CORN

4 C. corn
1 beaten egg
1 C. milk
16 saltine crackers
1 T. butter
1/4 onion, diced

SEASON WITH (to taste):
Mrs. Dash original blend
Mrs. Dash extra spicy
Salt and pepper

Mix all ingredients together in casserole dish. Add crackers to thickness desired. Bake 1 hour at 350°. Test with fork.

BROCCOLI CORN BAKE

1-1 lb. can cream-style corn
1-10 oz. box frozen chopped
  broccoli, cooked and drained
1 egg, beaten

1/2 C. coarse crushed saltine crackers
2 T. minced onion
1/2 tsp. salt
5 T. melted margarine

Combine corn, cooked broccoli, egg, cracker crumbs, onion, salt and melted margarine. Mix well. Pour into a greased 1-quart casserole. Top with crushed Ritz crackers and bake at 350° for 30 minutes.

CORN FRITTERS

1 1/3 C. flour
1 T. sugar
1 egg
1 C. whole corn, drained
2 tsp. baking powder

1/4 tsp. salt
1/2 C. milk
Powdered sugar
Syrup

Beat egg; add milk and blend in corn. Add dry ingredients and mix well. Drop by spoonfuls into deep fat (390°); fry until golden. Roll in powdered sugar. Put syrup over top and eat.

They don't reheat real well. Better to not use all mixture and refrigerate. I've been able to use it a couple days later.

FRIED EGGPLANT

Peel, slice 1/4" thick 1 medium eggplant. Dip slices in 1/3 cup evaporated milk.

COMBINE, DIP EGGPLANT IN:
1/4 C. cornmeal
1/4 C. flour

1/4 tsp. pepper
3/4 tsp. salt

Brown lightly in medium hot 1/4" deep oil. Serve immediately.

SLOW COOKER CASSOULET

1/2 C. chopped onion
1/2 C. thinly sliced carrots
1 lb. cocktail smoked sausages
16 oz. can baked beans
9 oz. pkg. frozen lima beans or
  16 oz. can lima beans, drained

8 oz. frozen green beans or 16 oz.
  can, drained
1/2 C. firmly packed brown sugar
1/2 C. ketchup
1 T. vinegar
1 tsp. prepared mustard

Combine all ingredients in slow cooker. Cook on high setting for 1 hour. Reduce heat to low and continue cooking for at least 5 hours, or bake in 350° oven in 3-quart casserole for 1 1/2 hours, stirring once after first 20 minutes.

GARDEN SMEDLEY

5 strips bacon, raw and diced
1 C. diced onion
4 cloves garlic, diced
1 C. okra, sliced
1 C. zucchini, diced

1 C. eggplant, diced
2 medium tomatoes, diced
Pepper to taste
Parmesan cheese

In a heavy frying pan, cook the bacon. Add to the bacon the onion and garlic and sauté until softened. Add the okra and zucchini and cook until tender. When the okra and zucchini are tender, add the eggplant and cook until it too is tender. Then add the tomatoes; cover and simmer for 2 to 3 minutes. Add the pepper to taste and sprinkle with Parmesan cheese. Serve immediately. For best color and greatest nutrition, leave the skins on all vegetables.

GREEN BEANS AND TOMATOES

2 strips bacon, diced
1/4 C. chopped onion
2 T. chopped green pepper
1 T. flour

2-17 oz. cans green beans, drained
1-16 oz. can tomatoes, drained
Salt and pepper to taste
Dash of garlic powder if desired

Fry bacon, onions and green pepper until brown and bacon is crisp. Add flour and stir. In 1 1/2-quart buttered casserole, combine tomatoes (break into pieces), green beans, seasonings, bacon mixture and bake at 325° until hot.

FRESH GREEN BEANS AND POTATOES

4 C. fresh green beans
2 C. cubed raw potatoes

6 or 8 bacon slices
2 tsp. salt

Combine green beans, potatoes, bacon which has been cut into 1" pieces in a saucepan. Add enough water to cover; add salt. Cook about 25 minutes or until vegetables are tender. Do not drain liquid.

SPANISH HOMINY

1 onion, finely chopped
1 bell pepper, finely chopped
1/4 C. bacon drippings or oil
2 to 3 tsp. chili powder
1-4 oz. can tomato paste

1-8 oz. can tomato sauce
1-4 oz. can mushrooms
Salt and pepper to taste
2-29 oz. cans hominy, drained
1 C. grated Cheddar cheese

Sauté onion and bell pepper in bacon drippings. Stir in chili powder. Add tomato paste, tomato sauce, mushrooms with liquid, salt and pepper. Mix hominy with the sauce. Pour into a buttered casserole and top with cheese. Bake at 325° F. for 25 minutes.

OKRA GUMBO

3 to 4 pieces of bacon
1 small-medium onion, chopped
2 C. sliced okra
2 C. fresh tomatoes (preferable) or
  2-16 oz. cans tomatoes, drained

1 tsp. Tabasco, optional
2 tsp. salt
1/4 tsp. sugar

Fry bacon in large skillet. Remove bacon and save 2 tablespoons bacon grease in skillet. Sauté chopped onion in bacon grease. Remove tops from okra and slice into about 1/2" slices. Add okra, tomatoes, Tabasco, salt and sugar and cook slowly for 25 to 30 minutes. Do not add water. Sprinkle bacon on top before serving.

Some of us treat our bodies as if
we had a spare in the trunk.

MARINATED VEGETABLES

2 carrots
2 bell peppers
3 ribs celery
2 medium onions

1 small head cauliflower
1 head broccoli
2 medium cucumbers
2 tomatoes

DRESSING:
1 1/4 C. vinegar
3 T. sugar

1 1/2 T. light olive oil

Wash, slice and mix all vegetables. Pour dressing over vegetables and store in refrigerator.

COUNTRY FRIED POTATOES

4 or 5 potatoes, sliced
1/2 C. shortening or oil
1 C. sliced onions

2 tsp. salt
1/4 tsp. black pepper

Heat shortening or oil in heavy skillet over low heat. Arrange a layer of sliced potatoes and sliced onion; repeat. Sprinkle with salt and pepper. Cover tightly. Cook over low heat for 15 minutes. Uncover and increase heat slightly and sauté for 10 minutes longer or until potatoes are crisp and brown on underside. Do not stir. Fold in half as with an omelet. Serve on a hot platter.

HASH BROWN POTATO CASSEROLE

2 lbs. thawed hash browns
1/2 C. melted margarine
1 tsp. salt
1/2 tsp. pepper

1/4 C. chopped onion
2 C. grated Cheddar cheese
1-12 oz. carton sour cream

Mix together. Pour into 9x13" pan. Top with 1/4 cup melted margarine and 3/4 cup crushed cornflakes or buttered bread crumbs. Bake for 45 minutes at 350°.

POTATO BROCCOLI BAKE

2 T. butter or margarine
2 T. all-purpose flour
1 tsp. salt
1/8 tsp. nutmeg
1/8 tsp. pepper
2 C. milk

13 oz. pkg. cream cheese
1/2 C. shredded process Swiss cheese
4 C. potatoes, cooked
1-10 oz. pkg. broccoli, cooked and
  drained
1/4 C. fine dry bread crumbs
1 T. butter or margarine, melted

Melt the 2 tablespoons butter; blend in flour and seasonings. Add milk; cook and stir until fluffy. Add cheeses, stirring until melted. Stir in potatoes. Turn half the mixture into 10x6x2" baking dish; top with broccoli. Spoon remaining mixture over and cover. Bake in 350° oven for 35 minutes. Add margarine and crumbs. Bake, uncovered, for 10 to 15 minutes.

NEW POTATOES

New potatoes (small red)
Chopped onion to taste
Chopped green pepper to taste

Garlic to taste
Sour cream, ranch dressing or French
  onion dip

Cut potatoes in half; put in skillet with water. Add onion, green pepper and garlic. Bring to boil. Cook, uncovered, until water is absorbed. Stir in sour cream, ranch dressing or French onion dip. Heat; serve.

SOUR CREAM POTATOES

1-26 oz. bag shredded hash browns
2 C. mild Cheddar cheese
1 onion, chopped
1 stick butter, melted
1 can cream of chicken soup
1-8 oz. sour cream

TOPPING:
1 C. cornflakes, crushed
1/4 C. butter, melted

Put hash browns, cheese and onion in a bowl. Mix together butter, chicken soup and sour cream. Pour over potatoes; stir. Put in 9x13" baking pan. Mix together topping and sprinkle over potatoes. Bake at 350° for 1 hour or more.

SCALLOPED POTATOES

1-20 oz. pkg. hash browns
1/2 C. butter, melted
Chopped onion if desired

1 C. sour cream
1 can cream of chicken soup
8 to 12 oz. pkg. shredded cheese

Put hash browns in 9x13" pan. Pour melted butter and onion over top. Mix together sour cream, chicken soup and most of shredded cheese. Pour over top of potatoes. Sprinkle with a little parsley and salt and pepper. Sprinkle remainder of cheese on top. Bake for 50 minutes in 350° oven.

SWEET POTATOES

6 or 7 large sweet potatoes
1 C. sour cream

2 T. brown sugar or to taste

Cook and mash sweet potatoes. Add sour cream and brown sugar. Salt and pepper to taste. Put in casserole; cover with large marshmallows. Bake at 325° for 25 minutes. Can be prepared ahead and then baked.

PRALINE YAMS

29 oz. can yams, drained
1/3 C. chopped pecans
1/3 C. coconut
1/3 C. firmly packed brown sugar

3 T. flour
3 T. butter or margarine, melted
Mini-marshmallows

Preheat oven to 350°. Place drained yams in ungreased 1 1/2-quart casserole or baking dish. In small bowl, combine remaining ingredients and blend well. Sprinkle over yams. Bake for 35 to 40 minutes until bubbly. Top with mini-marshmallows to cover. Cover and let set until marshmallows melt.

SPANISH RICE

1 small onion, chopped
1/4 C. chopped green pepper
3 T. butter

3 C. hot boiled rice
Salt and pepper to taste
1 1/4 C. canned tomatoes

Sauté onion and green pepper for 5 minutes in the butter. Add tomatoes and rice; heat to boiling. Then reduce heat and simmer for 6 minutes more. Season to taste.

SPINACH CASSEROLE

2 pkgs. frozen chopped spinach
1/2 tsp. sugar
3/4 can cream of mushroom soup

8 oz. grated Cheddar cheese
1 beaten egg
Salt
Bread crumbs

Partially cook spinach in small amount of salted water with 1/2 teaspoon sugar in it. Drain. Mix in soup, half the cheese, beaten egg and salt. Place in 1 1/2-quart buttered casserole. Top with remaining cheese and bread crumbs and bake at 350° for 45 minutes.

SKILLET SQUASH

1/4 C. margarine
1 T. dehydrated minced onion or
   1 medium onion, chopped
1/8 tsp. garlic powder
1/2 tsp. salt

1/8 tsp. pepper
5 medium yellow squash
1 C. grated Velveeta cheese
1 C. toasted bread crumbs

Melt margarine in electric skillet at 350°. Brown onion; add garlic powder, salt, and pepper. Slice squash into same skillet. Cook for 15 minutes or until tender. Sprinkle with cheese; top with bread crumbs.

CHILLED YELLOW SQUASH

5 medium yellow squash, thinly
   chopped
1/2 C. thinly sliced green onions
1/2 to 3/4 C. chopped green pepper
1/2 C. sliced celery
2 T. wine vinegar

3/4 C. sugar
1 tsp. salt
1/2 tsp. pepper
1/3 C. oil
2/3 C. vinegar
1 crushed clove garlic

Combine squash, onion, green pepper, celery and toss. Combine rest of ingredients together. Stir well and spoon over vegetables. Chill at least 12 hours, stirring occasionally. Drain and serve cold.

BAKED SQUASH CASSEROLE

4 medium yellow squash
Salt and pepper
3 beaten eggs

1 can potato soup, undiluted
1 C. grated Cheddar cheese, packed

Dice unpeeled squash. Boil in small amount of salted water until just tender. Drain well. Sprinkle with salt and pepper. Beat eggs. Combine squash with eggs, soup and cheese. Place in 10x6" buttered dish. Bake at 350° for 45 minutes.

STEWED ZUCCHINI

1 medium onion, diced (2/3 C.)
2 T. oil
1 lb. zucchini, cubed (3 C.)
1/4 tsp. pepper

1/2 tsp. salt
1/2 tsp. oregano
1 large tomato, chopped coarsely
  (2/3 C.)

In medium saucepan, sauté onion in oil a few minutes or until tender. Add zucchini; cover and cook over low heat, stirring occasionally, for 10 minutes or until crisp-tender. Add remaining ingredients; cook 2 minutes, or until heated through.

STUFFED ZUCCHINI

1 large zucchini, must be large
  enough to hold mixture you make
1 1/2 to 2 lbs. Italian sausage,
  browned

1 C. shredded Cheddar cheese, if
  desired
2 eggs
8 saltine crackers

Cut top 1/4 of zucchini off lengthwise. Scrape seeds out of center with a spoon. Fill hollow canal with sausage, egg and cracker mixture. Place in shallow baking dish. Bake at 325° until zucchini is tender. Test with fork.

I'm making my favorite thing for dinner
—reservations!

Has anyone seen Mom...

of course, she's <u>not</u> in the kitchen.

She'd rather dance on the dining room table with her grandkids than put a meal on it!

Desserts

ALMOND JOY CAKE

1 box chocolate cake mix with
   pudding
1 C. Pet milk
1 C. sugar
24 large marshmallows
1-14 oz. can Angel Flake coconut

1 1/2 C. sugar
1/2 C. Pet milk
1 stick oleo
1 1/2 C. chocolate chips
1 C. almonds, chopped

Mix cake mix as directed and bake 10 to 15 minutes in a 15x11x1" pan. Mix 1 cup Pet milk, sugar and marshmallows. Heat or microwave; then add coconut. Pour over cake while both are still hot. Mix remaining sugar, Pet milk and oleo. Bring to a boil. Then add chocolate chips. Stir until melted and add almonds. Pour over cake.

CARROT CAKE

1 3/4 C. flour
2 tsp. soda
2 tsp. cinnamon
1 tsp. salt
2 C. sugar
1 1/2 C. oil

4 eggs
2 tsp. vanilla
2 C. crushed carrots
8 oz. drained pineapple
1 C. flake coconut
1 C. pecans
1/2 C. raisins

Mix flour, soda, cinnamon and salt; set aside. Add dry ingredients to the sugar, oil, eggs and vanilla; mix well. Mix in the carrots, pineapple, coconut, pecans and raisins. Bake in 9x13" pan for 50 to 60 minutes. Frost with cream cheese frosting.

CREAM CHEESE FROSTING:
1-3 oz. pkg. cream cheese
1/4 C. margarine

1 tsp. vanilla
2 C. confectioners' sugar

Combine ingredients and beat by hand until smooth.

There's no sense in advertising your troubles
– there's no market for them!

WHITE CHOCOLATE CAKE

1 1/2 C. butter
3/4 C. water
1-4 oz. bar white chocolate
1 1/2 C. buttermilk
4 eggs, slightly beaten
1 1/2 tsp. vanilla extract

1/2 C. flour
3 C. flour
1 C. chopped pecans, toasted
2 1/4 C. sugar
1 1/2 tsp. baking soda

Combine butter and water in a medium saucepan. Bring to a boil over medium heat, stirring occasionally. Remove from heat. Add white chocolate pieces and stir until melted. Stir in buttermilk, eggs, and vanilla. Set aside. Combine 1/2 cup flour and pecans. Stir to coat. Set aside. Combine remaining 3 cups flour, sugar and soda in a large mixing bowl. Gradually stir in white chocolate mixture. Fold in pecan mixture. Batter will be thin. Pour into 3 greased and floured 9" round cake pans. Bake at 350° for 20 to 25 minutes. Cool in pans on wire rack for 10 minutes. Remove from pans and cool completely on wire racks.

WHITE CHOCOLATE ICING:
1-4 oz. bar white chocolate
1-8 oz. pkg. cream cheese, softened
1-3 oz. pkg. cream cheese, softened

1/3 C. butter, softened
6 1/2 C. sifted powdered sugar
1 1/2 tsp. vanilla extract

Melt white chocolate in a heavy saucepan over low heat, stirring constantly. Remove from heat; cool 10 minutes, stirring occasionally. Beat cream cheese and butter at medium speed until creamy, Gradually add white chocolate, beating constantly until blended. Gradually add powdered sugar and beat until smooth. Stir in vanilla.

No food tastes as good as the food you eat
when you're cheating on a diet.

CHOCOLATE SHEET CAKE

2 sticks margarine
1 C. water
4 T. cocoa
2 C. flour
2 C. sugar

1 tsp. baking soda
1/2 tsp. salt
2 beaten eggs
1/2 C. buttermilk

In saucepan, put margarine, water and cocoa. Bring to a hard boil. Take off heat. Have ready flour, sugar, baking soda and salt. Add to hot mixture. Mix beaten eggs with buttermilk. Blend all without mixer. Pour into floured and greased 9x13" pan and bake at 400° for 15 to 17 minutes.

ICING:
1 stick margarine
4 T. cocoa
6 T. milk

1 box confectioners' sugar
1 tsp. vanilla
1 C. chopped pecans

Bring margarine, cocoa, and milk to full boil. Remove from heat. Add sugar, vanilla, and nuts. If too thick, add a little milk. Pour over cake.

CHOCOLATE ZUCCHINI CAKE

1/2 C. margarine
1/2 C. oil
1 3/4 C. sugar
2 eggs
1 tsp. vanilla
1/2 C. milk
1/2 tsp. lemon juice

2 1/2 C. flour
1/2 tsp. baking powder
4 T. cocoa
1 tsp. salt
2 C. zucchini, grated
1/4 C. chocolate chips

Cream margarine, oil and sugar. Add 2 well-beaten eggs, vanilla, milk and lemon juice. Stir together and add to mixture; flour, baking powder, cocoa and teaspoon salt. When mixed, add finely chopped or grated zucchini. Pour into greased and floured 9x13" cake pan. Put chocolate chips on top. Bake at 325° for 40 to 45 minutes.

Silence is one of the greatest arts of conversation.

CRAZY CAKE

2 C. sugar
2 C. flour
1 C. butter
1 C. water
1/4 C. cocoa

2 eggs
1/2 C. milk
1 tsp. soda
1 tsp. vanilla

Mix sugar and flour; set aside. In a saucepan, melt together butter, water and cocoa. Pour over sugar and flour mixture; beat well. Add eggs, milk, soda and vanilla. Bake at 400° for 20 minutes. Cool and frost.

EARTHQUAKE CAKE

1 C. chopped pecans
1 C. coconut flakes
1 German chocolate cake mix
1-8 oz. cream cheese

1 stick butter
1 box powdered sugar
1 tsp. vanilla

Spray bottom of 9x13" pan with Pam. Pour pecans and coconut into pan and set aside. Prepare cake mix according to package directions. Pour over pecans and coconut. In a separate bowl, cream together the cream cheese, butter, powdered sugar and vanilla. Drop by spoonfuls over the raw cake batter. Bake at 350° for 45 to 50 minutes. Serve hot over ice cream.

FUNNEL CAKE

3 eggs
2 C. milk, heat until hot (may need
   1/4 to 1/2 C. after mixed to thin)

4 C. flour
1/4 C. honey
2 tsp. baking powder

Beat eggs, milk and honey. Sift flour and baking powder together. Add; beat mixture until smooth. Drop from funnel into 375° oil. If too thick, add 1/4 to 1/2 cup more milk. Fry until brown and drain. Sprinkle with powdered sugar.

KATHY'S STRAWBERRY CAKE

1 white cake mix
2 C. frozen or fresh strawberries

1 container Cool Whip

Make cake mix as directed. Let it fully cool. Spread strawberries over top. Spread Cool Whip over that. Serve cold.

KRAUT CHOCOLATE CAKE

2/3 C. butter or margarine
1 1/2 C. sugar
3 eggs
1 tsp. vanilla
1/2 C. unsweetened cocoa
2 1/4 C. sifted all-purpose flour

1 tsp. baking soda
1 tsp. baking powder
1/4 tsp. salt
1 C. water
2/3 C. rinsed, drained and chopped
  kraut

Cream butter with sugar. Beat in eggs and vanilla. Sift together dry ingredients. Add alternately with water to egg mixture. Stir in kraut. Turn into 2 greased and floured 8" square or round baking pans. Bake in 350° oven for 30 minutes or until cake tests done. Fill and frost with your favorite frosting.

POPPY SEED CAKE

3 beaten eggs
2 1/2 C. sugar
1 1/2 C. milk
1 C. plus 2 T. oil
1 1/2 tsp. almond extract
1 1/2 tsp. butter extract

1 1/2 tsp. vanilla extract
3 C. flour
1 1/2 tsp. salt
1 1/2 tsp. baking powder
2 T. poppy seed

GLAZE:
1/2 tsp. almond extract
1/4 C. orange juice

1/2 tsp. butter extract
3/4 C. sugar

Mix in order listed and pour into 2 loaf pans. Bake at 350° for 50 to 60 minutes. Pour glaze over loaves while hot.

Life is like a ladder.
Every step you take is either up or down.

RASPBERRY CREAM-FILLED CHOCOLATE CAKE

Preheat oven to 350°. Grease and flour standard size frying pan or cast iron skillet. Mix favorite chocolate cake. Pour into skillet or frying pan. Bake at 350° until cake pulls away from sides of pan and center bounces back from touch. Remove from oven; let cool 5 minutes. Remove cake from pan by inverting onto plate; set aside. RASPBERRY CREAM FILLING: In a large bowl, gently coat 2 cups raspberries with 1/2 cup sugar; set aside. Mix 1 package cream cheese (room temperature) with small carton whipped topping. Combine gently with raspberries; set aside. With long bread knife, slice cake into 2 layers; set aside top layer. Spread raspberry cream on bottom layer. Cover with top layer. Frost with favorite chocolate frosting. If desired, arrange additional raspberries on top. Drizzle with chocolate syrup. VARIATION: Use strawberries or cherries instead of raspberries.

SPRING BREEZE CHEESECAKE

1-8 oz. pkg. cream cheese, softened
1/3 C. sugar
1 C. sour cream
2 tsp. vanilla

1-8 oz. Cool Whip
1 Keebler Ready Crust (graham cracker crust)
Fresh strawberries for garnish

Beat cheese until smooth; gradually beat in sugar. Blend in sour cream and vanilla. Fold in Cool Whip, blending well. Spoon into pie crust. Chill until set, at least 4 hours. Garnish with fresh strawberries.

NO ROLL PIE CRUST

1 C. flour
1/2 C. soft margarine

1/4 C. powdered sugar

Heat oven to 400°. With hands, mix all ingredients to a soft dough. Press firmly and evenly against bottom and side of a 9" pie pan. Do not press on rim. Bake 12 to 15 minutes or until light brown. Cool. Do not bake first for a fruit pie. TO MAKE TOPPING FOR A FRUIT PIE: Add a little more flour and 1/4 cup additional sugar to above ingredients. Make the mixture into crumbs and spread on top of fruit. Bake complete pie.

BEST EVER PIE CRUST

3 C. sifted flour
1 C. lard or Crisco
1 T. vinegar

1 tsp. salt
1 beaten egg
Water

Sift flour and salt; add lard and work until mixture is like cornmeal. Break egg into cup. Beat up a little. Add vinegar and water to make 1/2 cup liquid. Sprinkle over flour mixture. Stir together and form into a ball. Chill for awhile. This makes 1 double crust. Roll to fit your pan.

EASY PIE CRUST

1 1/2 C. sifted flour
Dash of salt
1 T. sugar

1/2 C. salad oil
1/4 C. milk

Stir above ingredients as if mixing corn bread. Place in center of pie pan and pat into bottom and up onto sides. Makes 1 crust.

GRAHAM CRACKER PIE CRUST

1 C. graham cracker crumbs
1/3 C. margarine or butter, melted

1/4 C. sugar

Mix crumbs and sugar; blend in shortening. Press mixture into bottom and sides of 9" pie pan. Chill. Fill with your favorite pie filling. Sprinkle top with remainder pie crust mixture. Chill again before serving.

MERINGUE

3 egg whites
1/4 tsp. salt
1 tsp. lemon juice

1/4 tsp. vanilla
6 T. sugar

Add salt, vanilla and lemon juice to egg whites in mixing bowl. Beat until foamy. Add sugar 1 tablespoon at a time, beating constantly. Beat until sugar is dissolved and whites are glossy and stand in soft peaks. Pour hot filling into baked pie shell. Spread meringue on pie filling and seal the edge around the pie. Bake in 350° oven for 12 to 15 minutes.

APPLE PIE

6 to 8 good cooking apples, peeled
  and cored
1 tsp. cinnamon
1/2 tsp. nutmeg

Few drops of lemon juice
3 T. butter
Sugar to taste

Make pastry; line pie pan. Add sliced apples (previously mixed with sugar and spices). Put dabs of butter on top. Squeeze lemon juice over; cover with top crust. Puncture top with tines of fork. Bake at 350° for an hour.

BANANA CREAM PIE

1 to 2 bananas
1 baked 9" pie shell, cooled
2-4 serving size pkgs. vanilla or
  banana flavor instant pudding
  and pie filling

2 1/2 C. cold milk
2 C. thawed Cool Whip

Slice bananas into pie shell. Prepare pie filling mix as directed on package for pie, using 2 1/2 cups milk. Fold in 1/2 cup Cool Whip and pour over bananas in pie shell. Top with remaining Cool Whip. Chill at least 3 hours.

BISHOP CHOCOLATE PIE

1 box instant vanilla pudding
1 box instant milk chocolate
  pudding
2 C. milk

2 C. vanilla ice cream
Cool Whip
Graham cracker crust

Mix in order; pour in graham cracker crust. Put Cool Whip on top. Put in refrigerator.

CHOCOLATE CHIP PIE

1/4 C. plus 2 T. margarine, softened
1 C. sugar
1 tsp. vanilla
2 eggs
1/2 C. flour

1-6 oz. pkg. chocolate chips
3/4 C. pecans
1/2 C. coconut
1-9" pastry shell

Combine butter, sugar and vanilla in medium mixing bowl and beat well. Stir in flour. Gradually stir in chocolate chips, pecans and coconut. Pour mixture into pastry shell. Bake at 350° for 35 to 40 minutes.

COCONUT CREAM PIE

2 C. milk
2 T. cornstarch
1/4 tsp. salt
2/3 C. sugar

3 egg yolks
1 T. margarine
1 C. coconut

Bring to boil 1 1/2 cups milk. Blend the 1/2 cup milk with sugar, cornstarch, 3 yolks, and salt. Add this to the boiling milk. Add the margarine and the 2/3 cup coconut. Cool this; then spread into a baked lower pie crust. Make a meringue. Pile on top of the coconut filling. Dust with more coconut. Brown lightly in oven at about 350° for about 5 minutes or so.

GREEN TOMATO PIE

1 1/4 C. sugar
1/2 tsp. cinnamon
1/2 tsp. nutmeg
1/2 tsp. salt

5 T. flour
2 tsp. lemon juice
4 C. sliced green tomatoes, peeled
1-9" pie shell and crust

Combine dry ingredients. Add lemon juice and sliced tomatoes. Mix until tomatoes are well coated. Pour into pie shell and cover with crust. Bake for 1 hour at 425°.

KEY LIME PIE

COMBINE:
1-6 oz. can frozen lime juice
   concentrate

1 can Eagle Brand milk

Fold in 2 cups Cool Whip. Add several drops of green food coloring. Pour into graham cracker crust and freeze. After pie is frozen, slip into Ziploc bag. Pie can be kept in freezer for a month.
FOR LEMONADE PIE: Substitute a 6 ounce can frozen lemonade for lime juice and omit green food coloring.

Happiness is not something you find,
it's something you make.

LEMON MERINGUE PIE

1 C. sugar
1/4 C. cornstarch
1/4 tsp. salt
1 1/2 C. boiling water
2 egg yolks

1/3 C. lemon juice
1 tsp. grated rind of lemon
1 tsp. butter
1 baked pastry shell

Combine sugar, cornstarch and salt. Add water gradually and cook until smooth and thickened, stirring constantly. Cover and cook 15 minutes. Beat egg yolks and pour hot mixture over them gradually, stirring constantly. Cook 5 minutes longer. Just before removing from heat, add lemon juice, rind and butter. Mix well and cool. Pour into pastry shell. Top with meringue and proceed as directed. Makes 1-9" pie.

PECAN PIE

3 extra large eggs
1 C. sugar
1 C. white syrup
1 tsp. vanilla

2 T. melted butter
1/4 tsp. salt
1 C. chopped pecans

Beat eggs in blender. Add other ingredients except pecans one at a time, blending between each addition. Be careful not to over blend. It will make the filling bubbly. Place chopped pecans in the unbaked pie shell. Pour blended filling over pecans. Pecans will rise to the top. Bake at 325° for 45 minutes to 1 hour.

STRAWBERRY PIE

CRUST:
1/2 C. butter
1 C. flour

1/4 C. powdered sugar

Bake at 350° about 10 minutes or until brown.

GLAZE:
1 C. sugar
3 T. cornstarch

1 C. 7-Up

Boil until thick. May add red food coloring. Add 3 ounces strawberry jello; stir. Cool 5 minutes. Add strawberries on the top, about 1 pint.

FROZEN STRAWBERRY MARGARITA PIE

1 1/3 C. graham cracker crumbs
1/4 C. sugar
1/4 C. (1/2 stick) butter, melted
1-14 oz. can sweetened condensed
   milk
1/4 C. freshly squeezed lime juice

3 T. tequila
3 T. Triple-Sec
1/2 C. frozen strawberries with syrup,
   thawed
2 C. heavy cream, whipped

Combine crumbs, sugar and butter in a small bowl; press into bottom and sides of a 9" pie plate. Beat condensed milk, lime juice, tequila and Triple-Sec in a large bowl with electric mixer at medium speed for 3 minutes until smooth. Lower speed; beat in strawberries with syrup for 1 minute. Fold whipped cream into strawberry mixture until no streaks of white remain. Pour into prepared graham cracker pie shell, mounding in center. Freeze overnight. Transfer to refrigerator 30 minutes before serving. Garnish with additional whipped cream around edge, strawberries and lime slices, if you wish.

APPLE CRISP

1 C. sugar
1 C. flour
1 tsp. baking powder

1 egg
Apples, 6 to 7 large
Cinnamon

Peel and slice apples and spread in bottom of 9x13" cake pan. Sprinkle with cinnamon. Mix sugar, flour, baking powder then add egg; mix until crumbly. Spread over apple/cinnamon layer. Bake in moderate oven (approximately 350°) until apples are done and top is slightly browned. Other fresh fruit can be substituted for apples.

Worry is like a rocking chair;
it gives you something to do,
but doesn't get you anywhere.

APRICOT COBBLER

1 T. cornstarch
8 T. sugar
30 oz. can unpeeled apricot halves
   in heavy syrup
1 C. cake flour, fork-stir well to
   aerate before measuring

1 1/2 tsp. baking powder
1/2 tsp. salt
2 T. butter or margarine
6 T. milk

In a medium saucepan, stir together the cornstarch and 6 tablespoons of the sugar. Drain apricots; gradually stir 1 1/3 cups of the apricot syrup into the cornstarch mixture until smooth; add apricots. Cook over moderate heat, stirring constantly, until boiling and clear; keep hot. In a medium mixing bowl, stir together the flour, remaining 2 tablespoons sugar, baking powder, and salt. With a pastry blender, cut in butter until particles are fine. With a fork stir in milk, mixing as little as possible. Turn hot apricot mixture into an 8" square cake pan or dish. Drop batter from a teaspoon in 12 small mounds, spacing evenly, over hot apricot mixture. Bake in preheated 425° F. oven 25 to 30 minutes.

CAMP COBBLER

1 large can sliced peaches or 3 cups fresh peaches, peeled and sliced, simmered with 1 cup sugar for 3 to 5 minutes.
BATTER: Sift together 1 cup flour and 4 teaspoons baking powder. Add 1 cup sugar and 2/3 cup milk. Melt 1/2 cup butter in 6 1/2x10 1/2" Pyrex dish and pour the batter over it. Pour peaches and juice on top of batter. Do not mix. Bake at 350° for 30 minutes. When crust rises to top, sprinkle with sugar and bake 10 minutes longer.

FRUIT COBBLER QUICKIE
(ANY VARIETY)

2 to 3 C. fresh, frozen or canned
   fruit (peaches, plums, apricots,
   apples, or any other fruit you want
   to use)

1 C. sugar

Mix the above and let it stand. Melt 1/4 pound oleo in a 2-quart casserole in the oven. Mix 1 cup sugar, 1/4 teaspoon salt, 1 teaspoon baking powder, 3/4 cup flour and 3/4 cup milk and pour this batter over the melted oleo. Do not stir. Spoon the fruit over top of batter. Do not stir. Bake 45 minutes at 350°.

COCONUT CRUNCHIES

2 stick butter or margarine
1/2 C. sugar
1/2 C. brown sugar
1/2 tsp. vanilla
1 egg, beaten
1 C. flour

1/4 tsp. soda
1/2 tsp. baking powder
1/8 tsp. salt
1 C. oatmeal
1 C. cornflakes
1 C. coconut

Cream butter, sugars and vanilla. Add egg and mix until smooth. Sift dry ingredients together and add to first mixture. Mix in the oats, cornflakes and coconut. Drop by teaspoonful on a baking sheet. Bake at 325° for 15 to 20 minutes. Makes 4 dozen cookies.

CHOCOLATE CHIP PUDDING COOKIES

2 1/4 C. flour
1 tsp. baking soda
1 C. butter or margarine, softened
3/4 C. packed brown sugar
1/4 C. sugar

1-4 serving size pkg. instant chocolate
    pudding
1 tsp. vanilla
2 eggs
1-12 oz. pkg. chocolate chips
3/4 C. chopped nuts, optional

Mix flour with baking soda. Combine butter, sugars, pudding mix and vanilla. Beat in eggs. Gradually add flour mixture; then stir in chocolate chips and nuts. Batter will be stiff. Bake at 375° for 8 to 10 minutes on ungreased baking sheet. Do not overbake. Makes 7 dozen.

CHOCOLATE CHIP COOKIES

1 C. white sugar
1 C. brown sugar
1 C. margarine
1 C. oil
2 tsp. soda

4 tsp. cream of tartar
2 eggs
4 1/2 C. flour
Pinch of salt
1-12 oz. pkg. chocolate chips

Cream together the sugars, margarine and oil. Add the eggs; beat well. Mix in the flour, soda, cream of tartar and salt. Add the chocolate chips. Drop dough by teaspoon on ungreased cookie sheet. Bake in 350° oven for 10 minutes or until light brown.

KEY LIME WHITE CHOCOLATE COOKIES

1/3 C. margarine or butter, softened
3/4 C. packed brown sugar
2 T. granulated sugar
2 egg whites
1 1/2 tsp. vanilla

2 C. Bisquick
4 oz. white baking bars (white chocolate from 6 oz. pkg.) cut into chunks
1 T. grated lime peel

Heat oven to 350°. Beat margarine, sugars, egg whites and vanilla in large bowl on low speed until well mixed. Stir in remaining ingredients. Drop dough by rounded teaspoonfuls onto ungreased cookie sheet. Bake 8 to 10 minutes or until set but not brown. Cool 1 minute; remove from cookie sheet to wire rack. Makes about 3 dozen cookies.

COCONUT COOKIES

1/2 C. sugar
1 egg
1 tsp. vanilla
1/2 tsp. baking powder
1 C. flour
1/2 C. coconut

1/2 C. brown sugar
1/2 C. shortening
1/2 tsp. soda
1/2 tsp. salt
1 C. oatmeal
1/2 C. pecans

Blend sugar, brown sugar, egg, shortening and vanilla. Add remaining ingredients. Mix. Drop by spoon on cookie sheet. Bake at 375° for about 10 minutes.

DINOSAUR DIRT COOKIES

1/4 C. dirt (cocoa)
1/2 C. swamp water (water)
2 C. crushed bones (sugar)

1/2 C. fat (butter)
2 C. dried grass (oatmeal)
1/2 C. squashed bugs (peanut butter)

Mix the dirt and swamp water. Add bones and fat. Heat to boiling. Add the dry grass. Remove from heat and add the bugs. Mix and spoon onto waxed paper. Let cool and eat.

GRANDMA'S RAISIN COOKIES

1 1/2 C. shortening
1 C. brown sugar
1 C. white sugar
1 C. raisins
2 C. oatmeal
1 C. nuts

3 3/4 C. flour
3 eggs
1 tsp. vanilla
2 tsp. soda
Dash of salt

Mix ingredients together. Form into balls; roll in sugar and place on ungreased cookie sheet. Press flat with bottom of glass. Bake at 350° for 10 to 12 minutes.

NO BAKE COOKIES

4 T. cocoa
2 C. sugar
1 stick butter
1/2 C. milk

1 tsp. vanilla
2 1/2 C. oatmeal
1/2 C. peanut butter
Nuts, if desired

Boil cocoa, sugar, butter and milk; stir continuously 1 minute. NO LONGER. Remove from heat; add vanilla, oatmeal and peanut butter. With a regular cereal spoon, drop cookies onto wax paper. Let set until cool and firm.

PEANUT BUTTER COOKIES

1/2 C. shortening (I use butter or
    margarine)
1/2 C. peanut butter
1/2 C. granulated sugar
1/2 C. brown sugar, packed

1 egg
1 1/4 C. flour
1/2 tsp. baking powder
3/4 tsp. soda

Mix shortening, peanut butter, sugars and egg thoroughly. Measure flour, baking powder and soda together; blend. Stir flour mixture into peanut butter mixture. Roll dough into 1 1/4" balls. Place 3" apart on lightly greased baking sheet. Flatten crisscross style with fork dipped in flour. Bake at 375° for 10 minutes. Watch close. They burn easily. Makes about 3 dozen cookies.

PEANUT BUTTER CHOCOLATE CHIP COOKIES

1/2 C. margarine	1/2 tsp. vanilla
1/2 C. brown sugar	1/2 C. peanut butter
1/2 C. sugar	1 1/2 C. flour
2 eggs	1/2 tsp. soda
Salt	6 oz. chocolate chips

Cream margarine and sugars. Mix in remaining ingredients. Drop on cookie sheet. Bake at 350° until done.

BEST EVER SUGAR COOKIES

1 C. sugar	2 tsp. vanilla
1 C. powdered sugar	5 C. flour
1 C. margarine	1 tsp. soda
1 C. salad oil	1 tsp. cream of tartar
2 eggs, beaten	1/4 tsp. salt

Cream together sugars and butter. Combine with remaining ingredients; mix well. Roll into balls the size of a walnut. Place on cookie sheet 2" apart. Press with a glass dipped in sugar. Bake at 350° for 10 to 13 minutes.

SUGAR COOKIES

2 C. sugar	1 rounded tsp. baking powder
2 sticks oleo	1 tsp. salt
2 eggs	1 tsp. vanilla
1 C. sour cream	5 C. flour
2 level tsp. soda	

Cream together sugar and oleo. Add other ingredients and roll out on lots of flour to cut. Bake at 350° on ungreased pan for 10 to 12 minutes.

CHRISTMAS COOKIES

1/2 C. shortening	1 tsp. almond extract
1 C. sugar	2 3/4 C. flour
1 egg	1/2 tsp. soda
1/4 C. milk	1/2 tsp. baking powder

Cream shortening and sugar. Mix in egg, milk and almond. Add flour, soda and baking powder; chill overnight. Roll out on floured cloth and cut into cookies. Bake on ungreased cookie sheet at 375° for 8 to 10 minutes. Cool and frost or decorate.

BROWNIES

1 3/4 C. flour	1 tsp. vanilla
2 C. sugar	5 eggs
1/2 C. cocoa	1 C. Crisco oil
1 tsp. salt	

Mix all ingredients together, beating well. Pour in a greased 15 1/4x10" pan. Sprinkle 1/2 to 1 cup chips over the top and bake at 350° for 15 to 20 minutes. You can substitute peanut butter chips for chocolate if you wish.

BROWNIES

2 sticks margarine	2 C. flour
4 squares unsweetened chocolate	1 tsp. salt
2 C. sugar	1 tsp. baking powder
4 eggs	2 tsp. vanilla

Melt margarine and chocolate slowly. Beat sugar and eggs until light and fluffy. Add dry ingredients and vanilla to the sugar mixture; mix in chocolate and margarine. Pour into 9x13" pan and bake at 250° for 1 hour. Check with toothpick.

EASY BROWNIES

1/2 C. oleo or butter
1 1/2 C. brown sugar
1 tsp. vanilla
1 egg
1 tsp. salt

1/2 C. milk
1 1/2 C. flour
3 T. cocoa
1/2 tsp. soda
1/3 C. hot coffee

Mix oleo or butter, brown sugar, vanilla, egg and salt together. Add milk alternately with flour. Add cocoa and soda. Mix as a paste with hot coffee. Spread into 10x16" pan. Bake for 20 minutes in 350° oven. Ice with chocolate frosting.

HERSHEY BROWNIES

1 stick oleo
1 C. sugar
4 eggs

1 C. flour
1 can Hershey's syrup

Cream together softened oleo and sugar; add eggs, one at a time. Add flour and mix well. Pour into Hershey's syrup. Pour batter into pan; bake at 350° for 25 to 30 minutes or until cake springs back. Sprinkle powdered sugar over for frosting.

BANANA BARS

4 bananas, cut in chunks
1 tsp. soda
1 1/2 C. sugar
1 C. oil
2 eggs, beaten

2 C. flour
1 tsp. vanilla
1/2 C. nuts
Pinch of salt

Mix all ingredients. Bake in 13x9" pan at 325° for 35 minutes. Cool and cut in bars.

*Real discipline is when you can pick
strawberries without eating any.*

CREAM CHEESE BARS

2-8 oz. tubes crescent rolls
2-8 oz. pkgs. cream cheese
1 C. sugar
1 tsp. vanilla
1 egg
1 tsp. lemon juice

TOPPING:
1/2 C. sugar
1/2 C. flour
1/4 C. melted butter

Grease 9x13" pan. Line with 1 package of rolls. Beat next five ingredients together. Spread over rolls. Layer second package of rolls over cream cheese mixture. Sprinkle topping over crescent rolls. Bake at 350° for 30 to 35 minutes.

MOUND BARS

2 C. graham cracker crumbs
1/2 C. butter, melted
1/2 C. sugar
2 C. Angel Flake coconut

1 C. sweetened condensed milk
1 large pkg. chocolate chips
1 large pkg. butterscotch chips

Mix graham cracker crumbs, butter and sugar. Line bottom of 9x13" pan and bake for 10 minutes. Combine condensed milk and coconut; spread over crust. Bake at 350° for 10 minutes. Melt chocolate and butterscotch chips and spread on warm bars. Tastes just like the candy bar. (I use chocolate graham crackers.

PUMPKIN BARS

2 C. sugar
4 eggs
1/2 tsp. salt
2 tsp. baking powder
1 tsp. cinnamon
1 C. oil
2 C. pumpkin
2 C. flour
1 tsp. soda

FROSTING:
3 oz. cream cheese
3 C. powdered sugar
3/4 stick oleo
1 tsp. vanilla

Mix in order. Bake at 325° for 30 minutes in a 10x13" jelly roll pan. Cool completely before frosting.
FROSTING: Cream all ingredients together until well blended.

TWIX BARS

Club crackers
1 C. graham cracker crumbs
3/4 C. brown sugar
1/2 C. white sugar

1/3 C. milk
1/2 C. margarine
2/3 C. peanut butter
1 C. chocolate chips

Place one layer of Club crackers on the bottom of a buttered 9x13" pan. Stir together graham cracker crumbs, brown sugar, white sugar, milk and margarine. Boil for 5 minutes. Pour mixture over crackers; then place another layer of Club crackers over that. Melt peanut butter and chocolate chips. Spread this over all. Refrigerate.

BANANA SPLIT DESSERT

1ST LAYER:
2 C. graham cracker crumbs
1/4 C. sugar
1 stick melted butter
2ND LAYER:
8 oz. cream cheese
1 tsp. vanilla
1 C. powdered sugar
12 oz. Cool Whip

3RD LAYER:
2 C. crushed pineapple, well drained
3 to 4 bananas

4TH LAYER:
Chocolate syrup
Maraschino cherries
1 C. chopped nuts

1ST LAYER: Mix graham cracker crumbs, melted butter and sugar together. Spread in a 13x9" pan.
2ND LAYER: Whip cream cheese, powdered sugar and vanilla together. Fold in Cool Whip. Save back 2 cups of mixture and spread rest of mixture on top of first layer.
3RD LAYER: Spread pineapple on top of second layer. Slice bananas on top of pineapple. Cover with remaining cheese mixture.
4TH LAYER: Drizzle top with chocolate syrup. Sprinkle with nuts and place cherries on top. I always put one for each serving section. Keep refrigerated until ready to serve.

*Middle age is when the phone rings
and you hope it's not for you.*

BANANA SPLIT

3 C. crushed graham crackers
3 or 4 bananas
1/2 gal. Neapolitan ice cream
1 C. chocolate chips

1/2 C. margarine
12 oz. evaporated milk
2 C. powdered sugar
1 tsp. vanilla

Crush 3 cups of graham crackers and put in bottom of 9x12" cake pan. Cover with 3 or 4 sliced bananas. Put 1/2 gallon sliced Neapolitan ice cream over bananas. Melt 1 cup chocolate chips and 1/2 cup margarine together. Add can evaporated milk and 2 cups powdered sugar. Cook until thick. Add 1 teaspoon vanilla. Cool and spread over Neapolitan ice cream. Cover and freeze. Delicious holiday treat!

BLACKBERRY PUDDING

1 qt. fresh blackberries (canned
  may be used, but not as good)

1 beaten egg
2 T. flour
Pinch salt

Stir and chop ingredients together. Cook in double boiler covered, about 45 minutes. Stir often.

SAUCE:
3/4 C. brown sugar
2 T. melted butter

1 tsp. boiling water
Dash nutmeg

Mix ingredients together. Pudding and sauce may be served hot or cold.

BLUEBERRY DELIGHT

24 squares or 1 pkg. (12) graham
  crackers
2 pkgs. Dream Whip
1 C. cold milk

1 tsp. vanilla
1 C. powdered sugar
1-8 oz. pkg. cream cheese
1 can blueberries, drain off juice

Roll crackers and put half in bottom of cake pan. Mix 2 packages Dream Whip with 1 cup milk and vanilla in large bowl. Beat until thick; add powdered sugar and cream cheese (at room temperature). Beat together until real stiff. Put half on top of the cracker crumbs in pan. Put can of berries on next, then rest of Dream Whip mix. Sprinkle rest of cracker crumbs on top. Put in refrigerator. Will keep a long time if kept chilled.

BLUEBERRY JELLO DESSERT

JELLO MIX:
1 large box jello, cherry or
   strawberry
16 oz. can blueberry pie filling

15 oz. can crushed pineapple
1 C. chopped pecans

Dissolve jello in 2 cups boiling water. Add blueberries and pineapple with juice. Add pecans and mix well. Chill until firm.

TOPPING:
8 oz. cream cheese
8 oz. Cool Whip
8 oz. sour cream

1/2 C. sugar
1 tsp. vanilla

Whip together. After jello is set, top with topping.

CHERRIES IN THE SNOW

1-8 oz. pkg. cream cheese, softened
1 C. powdered sugar
1 angel food cake, sliced thinly
1 C. milk

1 box (2 pkgs.) Dream Whip
1 tsp. vanilla
1 can cherry pie filling

Prepare Dream Whip as package directions (1 cup milk and 1 teaspoon vanilla). Mix softened cream cheese and powdered sugar. Add to Dream Whip mixture. Put light layer of cream cheese mixture in bottom of dish. Next layer, add cake slices, then another layer of cream cheese mixture. Repeat again. End up with a layer of angel food cake, then spread the cherry pie filling. Refrigerate.

CHERRY WHIP

2-21 oz. cans cherry pie filling
1 large tub Cool Whip
1 large box vanilla pudding mixed
   according to directions

1 small bag colored marshmallows
3 to 4 bananas

Mix all ingredients together except bananas; cool. Just before serving, add bananas.

CHOCOLATE BREAD PUDDING

2-1 oz. squares unsweetened
  chocolate
2 C. lightly packed torn bread pieces

2 C. milk
1 C. sugar
1 slightly beaten egg
1 tsp. vanilla

Put chocolate in saucepan with bread, milk and sugar. Cook over low heat until chocolate melts. Remove from heat and add egg and vanilla. Bake at 350° for 45 to 60 minutes. Serve warm with hard sauce or whipped cream. Serves 4 to 6.

HARD SAUCE:
1/2 stick butter
1 C. sifted confectioners' sugar

1/2 tsp. vanilla

Soften butter in small bowl; then cream butter and gradually add sugar, creaming while adding. Add vanilla. Serve generously as dollops on Chocolate Bread Pudding.

HOLLY

46 large marshmallows
1 stick margarine
1 1/2 tsp. green food coloring

3 1/2 C. cornflakes
Red cinnamon drops

Melt marshmallows and butter over low heat. Add food coloring until dark green, then fold in cornflakes gently. Drop by teaspoons onto buttered cookie sheet or waxed paper. Put cinnamon drops on right away. Let cool in refrigerator.

GOLDEN RULES FOR LIVING
If you open it, close it,
If you turn it on, turn if off.
If you unlock it, lock it up.
If you break it, admit it.
If you can't fix it, call in someone who can.
If you borrow it, return it.
If you value it, take care of it.
If you make a mess, clean it up.
If you move it, put it back.

OLD-FASHIONED ICEBOX DESSERT

15 Honey Maid honey grahams
1-8 oz. pkg. Philadelphia cream
cheese, softened
3 C. milk

1-4 serving size pkg. jello vanilla flavor
instant pudding and pie filling
1-8 oz. tub Cool Whip whipped topping,
thawed, divided
1/2 C. toasted Baker's Angle Flake
coconut

Arrange grahams in bottom of 13x9" pan; set aside. Beat cream cheese in large
bowl with electric mixer until smooth; gradually blend in milk. Add pudding mix;
beat 1 minute. Fold in half of the topping. Spread pudding mixture in prepared
pan. Spread remaining whipped topping over pudding layer. Refrigerate at least 2
hours or overnight. To serve, top with coconut. Cut into squares. Makes 15 servings.

Make this ahead and store it in your icebox or refrigerator.

SALTED NUT ROLL BARS

1 can sweetened condensed milk
1-12 oz. pkg. Reese's peanut butter
chips

3 C. miniature marshmallows
2-12 oz. jars salted or dry roasted
peanuts

Melt condensed milk, peanut butter chips and marshmallows in the microwave for
about 2 1/2 minutes. Spread 1 jar of peanuts in a 9x13" pan. Spread melted
ingredients over peanuts. Top with remaining jar of peanuts. Refrigerate.

PEANUT BUTTER FUDGE

2/3 C. evaporated milk
2 C. sugar
1 C. crunchy peanut butter

2 C. marshmallow creme
1 tsp. vanilla

Cook milk and sugar to 234°, stirring occasionally. Remove from heat and add
peanut butter, marshmallow creme and vanilla. Beat until smooth. Pour into a
buttered pan.

PEANUT CLUSTERS

1/3 C. margarine
1-6 oz. pkg. milk chocolate morsels
1-4 oz. pkg. full-sized marshmallows

1/2 tsp. vanilla
2 C. salted peanuts

Place margarine, chocolate morsels and 16 marshmallows in saucepan. Heat over medium heat and stir until chocolate and marshmallows are melted; add vanilla. Remove from heat and stir in peanuts. Cover 2 cookie sheets with Reynolds Wrap and drop by rounded teaspoonfuls of mixture on foil. Chill in refrigerator until hard. Yield: 2 dozen clusters.

RHUBARB CRUNCH

Rhubarb
1 C. oatmeal
1 C. flour
1 C. brown sugar, packed
1/2 C. butter or margarine

1 C. sugar
1 C. water
3 T. cornstarch
1 tsp. vanilla

Mix oatmeal, flour, brown sugar and butter. Spread half of mixture in bottom of 8x8" pan. Boil sugar, water and cornstarch together until thick. Add vanilla. Place rhubarb evenly in lined pan and pour cooked mixture over rhubarb. Sprinkle rest of crumb topping over all. Bake at 350° for 1 hour. Double recipe for 8 1/2x11" pan. Load down with rhubarb.

THE THING

1 box cake mix, any flavor
1 stick butter

1 C. chopped nuts
1 egg

Cut above ingredients together and press in pan.

TOPPING:
8 oz. cream cheese
2 eggs

1 lb. powdered sugar

Mix with mixer. Pour on top of cake mixture. Bake at 350° for 35 minutes.

THREE LAYER DESSERT

1ST LAYER:
1 1/2 C. flour   3/4 C. chopped nuts
3/4 C. butter

Mix; press into 9x13" pan. Bake at 350° for 10 minutes. Cool.

2ND LAYER:
1 large (8 oz.) pkg. cream cheese   1 C. Cool Whip
1 C. powdered sugar

Stir Cool Whip into cheese and sugar.

3RD LAYER:
2 pkgs. instant coconut pudding or   3 C. milk
  pistachio

Mix as usual and pour on top. Top with Cool Whip and nuts (optional).

If it belongs to someone else, get permission to use it.
If you don't know how to operate it,
leave it alone.
If it's none of your business, don't ask questions.

About the author

Pete Wilde

**Let's just say this ~
He's smiling in this
1969 photograph because
he doesn't yet realize
how many meals he will have to
cook in the next 35 years.**

The women finally let us take a break!

The End

INDEX

APPETIZERS & DRINKS

BREADS, SWEET BREADS & BRUNCH

SOUPS, SALADS & SANDWICHES

MAIN DISHES, MEAT & WILD GAME

v

VEGETABLES

DESSERTS

"HOUSEHOLD HINTS"

Tips to remedy this or that in the household

TABLE OF CONTENTS

COMMON KITCHEN PANS TO USE

WHEN THE RECIPE CALLS FOR:
4-cup baking dish:
9-inch pie plate
8 x 1 1/4-inch layer cake pan - C
7 3/8 x 3 5/8 x 2 1/4-inch loaf pan - A
6-cup baking dish:
8 or 9 x 1 1/2-inch layer-cake pan - C
10-inch pie plate
8 1/2 x 3 5/8 x 2 5/8-inch loaf pan - A
8-cup baking dish:
8 x 8 x 2-inch square pan - D
11 x 7 x 1 1/2-inch baking pan
9 x 5 x 3-inch loaf pan - A
10-cup baking dish:
9 x 9 x 2-inch square pan
11 3/4 x 7 1/2 x 1 3/4-inch baking pan - D
15 x 10 x 1-inch jellyroll pan
12-cup baking dish or over:
12 1/3 x 8 1/2 x 2-inch glass baking pan -   12 cups
13 x 9 x 2-inch metal baking pan -   15 cups
14 x 10 1/2 x 2 1/2-inch roasting -   19 cups

TOTAL VOLUME OF VARIOUS SPECIAL BAKING PANS
Tube Pans:
7 1/2 x 3-inch "Bundt" tube - K -   6 cups
9 x 3 1/2-inch fancy tube or "Bundt" pan - J or K - 9 cups
9 x 3 1/2-inch angel cake pan - H -   12 cups
10 x 3 3/4-inch "Bundt" or "Crownburst" pan - K - 12 cups
9 x 3 1/2-inch fancy tube - J -   12 cups
10 x 4-inch fancy tube mold (kugelhupf) - J -   16 cups
10 x 4-inch angel cake pan - H -   18 cups
Spring-Form Pans:
8 x 3-inch pan - B -   12 cups
9 x 3-inch pan - B -   16 cups
Ring Mold:
8 1/2 x 2 1/4-inch mold - E -   4 1/2 cups
9 1/4 x 2 3/4-inch mold - E -   8 cups
Charlotte Mold:
6 x 4 1/4-inch mold - G -   7 1/2 cups
Brioche Pan:
9 1/2 x 3 1/4-inch pan - F -   8 cups

A

B

C

D

E

F

G

H

J

K

QUANTITIES TO SERVE 100 PEOPLE

Coffee .... 3 lbs.	Bread .... 10 loaves
Cream .... 3 qts.	Rolls 200
Whipping cream .... 4 pts.	Butter .... 3 lbs.
Milk .... 6 gallons	Potato salad .... 3 1/2 to 4 gals.
Fruit cocktail .... 2 1/2 gallons	Fruit salad .... 20 qts.
Fruit juice .... 4 #10 cans	Vegetable salad .... 20 qts.
Tomato juice .... 4 #10 cans	Lettuce .... 16 lg. heads
Soup .... 5 gallons	Salad dressing .... 3 qts.
Hot Dogs .... 25 lbs.	Jello .... 2 1/2 qts.
Meat loaf .... 18 to 22 lbs.	Pies 18
Ham .... 40 lbs.	Cakes 8
Beef .... 40 lbs.	Ice Cream .... 4 gallons
Roast pork .... 40 lbs.	Cheese .... 3 lbs.
Hamburger .... 30 to 36 lbs.	Olives .... 1 3/4 lbs.
Chicken for chicken pie .... 40 lbs.	Pickles .... 2 qts.
Potatoes .... 35 lbs.	Nuts .... 3 lbs.
Scalloped potatoes .... 4 gals.	
Spaghetti .... 5 gals.	
Vegetables .... 4 #10 cans	
Baked beans .... 5 gals.	
Beets .... 25 lbs.	
Cauliflower .... 18 lbs.	
Cabbage for slaw .... 16 lbs.	
Carrots .... 24 lbs.	
Corn .... 2 #10 cans	

To serve 50 people, divide by 2. To serve 25 people, divide by 4.

Cooking for a crowd. The season of the year rules the food choices to a degree. Also variety in flavor, texture, color and form. Plan best use of refrigerator space. Decide type of service, buffet, family style or served plates with waitresses.

CONTENTS OF CANS

Of the different sizes of cans used by commercial canners, the most common are:

Size	Average Contents
8 ounces	1 cup
picnic	1 1/4 cups
No. 300	1 3/4 cups
No. 1 tall	2 cups
No. 303	2 cups
No. 2	2 1/2 cups
No. 2 1/2	3 1/2 cups
No. 3	4 cups
No. 10	12 to 13 cups

SUBSTITUTIONS

FOR: **YOU CAN USE:**

1 T. cornstarch .... 2 T. flour OR 1 1/2 T. quick cooking tapioca

1 C. cake flour .... 1 C. less 2 T. all-purpose flour

1 C. all-purpose flour .... 1 C. plus 2 T. cake flour

1 square chocolate .... 3 T. cocoa and 1 T. fat

1 C. melted shortening .... 1 C. salad oil (may not be substituted for solid shortening)

1 C. milk .... 1/2 C. evaporated milk and 1/2 C. water

1 C. sour milk or buttermilk .... 1 T. lemon juice or vinegar and enough sweet milk to measure 1 C.

1 C. heavy cream .... 2/3 C. milk and 1/3 C. butter

1 C. heavy cream, whipped....... 2/3 C. well-chilled evaporated milk, whipped

Sweetened condensed milk ...... No substitution

1 egg .... 2 T. dried whole egg and 2 T. water

1 tsp. baking powder .... 1/4 tsp. baking soda and 1 tsp. cream of tartar OR 1/4 tsp. baking soda and 1/2 C. sour milk buttermilk or molasses; reduce other liquid 1/2 C.

1 C. sugar................................. 1 C. honey; reduce other liquid 1/4 C.; reduce baking temperature 25°

1 C. miniature marshmallows .... About 10 large marshmallows, cut up

1 medium onion (2 1/2" dia.) ..... 2 T. instant minced onion OR 1 tsp. onion powder OR 2 tsp. onion salt; reduce salt 1 tsp.

1 garlic clove .... 1/8 tsp. garlic powder OR 1/4 tsp. garlic salt reduce salt 1/8 tsp.

1 T. fresh herbs .... 1 tsp. dried herbs OR 1/4 tsp. powdered herbs OR 1/2 tsp. herb salt; reduce salt 1/4 tsp.

SUBSTITUTIONS

For bread crumbs: Use crushed corn or wheat flakes, or other dry cereal. Or use potato flakes.

For butter: Use 7/8 cup of solid shortening plus 1/2 teaspoon of salt.

For fresh milk: To substitute 1 cup of fresh milk, use 1/2 cup each of evaporated milk and water.

For 1 cup of whole milk, prepare 1 liquid cup of nonfat dry milk and 2 1/2 teaspoons butter or margarine.

For sugar: Use brown sugar, although it will result in a slight molasses flavor.

For superfine sugar: Process regular granulated sugar in your blender.

For red and green sweet pepper: Use canned pimientos.

For vanilla extract: Use grated lemon or orange rind for flavoring instead. Or try a little cinnamon or nutmeg.

For flour: Use 1 tablespoon cornstarch instead of 2 tablespoons of flour. Or try using instant potatoes or cornmeal.

For buttermilk: Use 1 tablespoon of lemon juice or vinegar and enough fresh milk to make 1 cup. Let it stand 5 minutes before using.

For catsup: Use a cup of tomato sauce added to 1 1/4 cups of brown sugar, 2 tablespoons of vinegar, 1/4 teaspoon of cinnamon and a dash of ground cloves and allspice.

For unsweetened chocolate: Use 1 tablespoon of shortening plus 3 tablespoons of unsweetened chocolate to equal 1 square of unsweetened chocolate.

For corn syrup: Use 1/4 cup of water or other type of liquid called for in the recipe, plus 1 cup of sugar.

For eggs: Add 3 or 4 extra tablespoons of liquid called for in the recipe. Or, when you're 1 egg shy for a recipe that calls for many, substitute 1 teaspoon of cornstarch.

For cake flour: Use 7/8 cup of all-purpose flour for each cup of cake flour called for in a recipe.

For fresh herbs and spices: For 1/3 the amount of dried herbs or spices. Dried herbs are more concentrated.

For honey: To substitute 1 cup of honey, use 1 1/4 cups of sugar and 1/4 cup of water or other liquid called for in the recipe.

DEEP-FAT FRYING TEMPERATURES WITHOUT A THERMOMETER

A 1-inch cube of white bread will turn golden brown:

345° to 355°	65 seconds
355° to 365°	60 seconds
365° to 375°	50 seconds
375° to 385°	40 seconds
385° to 395°	20 seconds

OVEN TEMPERATURES

Slow	300°
Slow moderate	325°
Moderate	350°
Quick moderate	375°
Moderately hot	400°
Hot	425°
Very Hot	475°

SIMPLIFIED MEASURES

Measure	Equivalent
1 tablespoon	3 teaspoons
2 tablespoons	1 ounce
1 jigger	1 1/2 ounces
1/4 cup	4 tablespoons
1/3 cup	5 tablespoons plus 1 teaspoon
1/2 cup	8 tablespoons
1 cup	16 tablespoons
1 pint	2 cups
1 quart	4 cups
1 gallon	4 quarts
1 liter	4 cups plus 3 tablespoons
1 ounce (dry)	2 tablespoons
1 pound	16 ounces
2.21 pounds	35.3 ounces

FOOD GUIDE PYRAMID

A Guide to Daily Food Choices

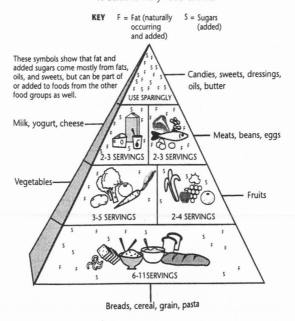

KEY   F = Fat (naturally   S = Sugars
             occurring   (added)
             and added)

These symbols show that fat and added sugars come mostly from fats, oils, and sweets, but can be part of or added to foods from the other food groups as well.

USE SPARINGLY

Candies, sweets, dressings, oils, butter

Milk, yogurt, cheese

2-3 SERVINGS

Meats, beans, eggs

2-3 SERVINGS

Vegetables

3-5 SERVINGS

Fruits

2-4 SERVINGS

6-11 SERVINGS

Breads, cereal, grain, pasta

EQUIVALENTS FOR COMMON COOKING INGREDIENTS

1 lb.	**Apples**	3 or 4 medium
1 lb.	**Bananas**	3 or 4 medium
1 lb.	**Beans, dried**	5 to 6 cups cooked
1 quart	**Berries**	3 1/2 cups
1 slice	**Bread**	1/2 cup crumbs
1/4 lb.	**Cheese, grated**	1 cup
1 oz.	**Chocolate, 1 square**	1 T. melted
1/2 pint	**Cream**	1 cup
1 cup	**Cream, heavy**	2 cups whipped
1 lb.	**Flour, all-purpose**	4 cups sifted
1 envelope	**Gelatin**	1 T.
1 tsp.	**Herbs, dried**	1 T. fresh
2-3 T. juice	**Lemon**	1 1/2 tsp. grated rind
1 cup dry	**Macaroni**	2 1/4 cups cooked
1 lb.	**Meat, diced**	2 cups
1 lb.	**Mushrooms**	5-6 cups sliced
1/4 lb.	**Nuts, shelled**	1 cup chopped
1 medium	**Onion**	1/2 cup chopped
6-8 T. juice	**Orange**	1/3-1/2 cup pulp
3 medium	**Potatoes**	1 3/4 - 2 cups mashed
1 cup uncooked	**Rice**	3 cups cooked
1/2 lb.	**Spaghetti**	3 1/2 - 4 cups cooked
1 lb.	**Sugar, confectioners**	4 1/2 cups unsifted
1 lb.	**Sugar, granulated**	2 cups
1 lb.	**Tomatoes**	3 or 4 medium
1 lb.	**Walnuts in shell**	1 3/4 cups chopped

COMMON CAUSES OF FAILURE IN BAKING

BISCUITS

1. Rough biscuits caused from insufficient mixing.
2. Dry biscuits caused from baking in too slow an oven and handling too much.
3. Uneven browning caused from cooking in dark surface pan (use a cookie sheet or shallow bright finish pan), too high a temperature and rolling the dough too thin.

MUFFINS

1. Coarse texture caused from insufficient stirring and cooking at too low a temperature.
2. Tunnels in muffins, peaks in center and soggy texture are caused from overmixing.
3. For a nice muffin, mix well but light and bake at correct temperature.

CAKES

1. Cracks and uneven surface may be caused by too much flour, too hot an oven and sometimes from cold oven start.
2. Cake is dry may be caused by too much flour, too little shortening, too much baking powder or cooking at too low a temperature.
3. A heavy cake means too much sugar has been used or baked too short a period.
4. A sticky crust is caused by too much sugar.
5. Coarse grained cake may be caused by too little mixing, too much fat, too much baking powder, using fat too soft, and baking at too low a temperature.
6. Cakes fall may be caused by using insufficient flour, under baking, too much sugar, too much fat or not enough baking powder.
7. Uneven browning may be caused from cooking cakes at too high a temperature, crowding the shelf (allow at least 2" around pans) or using dark pans (use bright finish, smooth bottomed pans).

8. Cake has uneven color is caused from not mixing well. Mix thoroughly, but do not over mix.

PIES

1. Pastry crumbles caused by overmixing flour and fat.
2. Pastry is tough caused by using too much water and over mixing dough.
3. Pies do not burn - for fruit or custard pies use a Pyrex pie pan or enamel pan and bake at 400° to 425° constant temperature.

BREADS (YEAST)

1. Yeast bread is porous - this is caused by over-rising or cooking at too low a temperature.
2. Crust is dark and blisters - this is caused by over-rising, the bread will blister just under the crust.
3. Bread does not rise - this is caused from over-kneading or from using old yeast.
4. Bread is streaked - this is caused from underkneading and not kneading evenly.
5. Bread baked uneven - caused by using old dark pans, too much dough in pan, crowding the oven shelf or cooking at too high temperature.

WHAT TO USE SPICES AND SEASONINGS FOR!

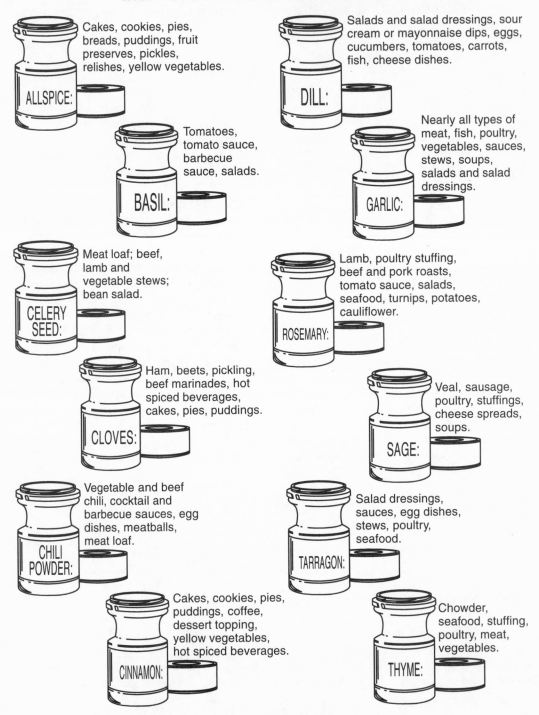

ALLSPICE: Cakes, cookies, pies, breads, puddings, fruit preserves, pickles, relishes, yellow vegetables.

DILL: Salads and salad dressings, sour cream or mayonnaise dips, eggs, cucumbers, tomatoes, carrots, fish, cheese dishes.

BASIL: Tomatoes, tomato sauce, barbecue sauce, salads.

GARLIC: Nearly all types of meat, fish, poultry, vegetables, sauces, stews, soups, salads and salad dressings.

CELERY SEED: Meat loaf; beef, lamb and vegetable stews; bean salad.

ROSEMARY: Lamb, poultry stuffing, beef and pork roasts, tomato sauce, salads, seafood, turnips, potatoes, cauliflower.

CLOVES: Ham, beets, pickling, beef marinades, hot spiced beverages, cakes, pies, puddings.

SAGE: Veal, sausage, poultry, stuffings, cheese spreads, soups.

CHILI POWDER: Vegetable and beef chili, cocktail and barbecue sauces, egg dishes, meatballs, meat loaf.

TARRAGON: Salad dressings, sauces, egg dishes, stews, poultry, seafood.

CINNAMON: Cakes, cookies, pies, puddings, coffee, dessert topping, yellow vegetables, hot spiced beverages.

THYME: Chowder, seafood, stuffing, poultry, meat, vegetables.

WHICH APPLES ARE BEST?

BAKING: Albermarle Pippin, Granny Smith, Jonathan, Rome Beauty
EATING: Red and Yellow Delicious, Grimes Golden, Rome Beauty
PIE: Granny Smith, Grimes Golden, Rome Beauty, Stayman, Winesap
SALAD: Granny Smith, Grimes Golden, Red Delicious, Rome Beauty, York Imperial, Winesap
SAUCE: Early Harvest, Summer Rambo, Grimes Golden, Stayman, Winesap, York Imperial

APPLES

• Place apple cider in 32 cup percolator coffeemaker and fill coffee basket 1/2 full of red-hot candies. Makes tasty spicy pink cider.
• Premeasure and freeze apple slices for Apple Crisp recipes.
• Substitute apples for blueberries in muffins.
• Put 2 tablespoons apple juice concentrate in cream cheese frosting for applesauce cupcakes.
• Keep apples from absorbing strong refrigerator odors by storing them in a plastic bag. They will stay fresher longer and won't speed ripening of other produce.
• Toss lemon juice on cut-up apples to prevent browning.
• Add 1/2 cup extra apples to a pie that you wish "very full".
• Cut apple in half horizontally. Cut design in apple halves and use for stamps to decorate. Kids love this!

BARBECUES

• It's simple to grill acorn squash. Pierce the skin with fork a couple of times, then wrap in aluminum foil. Grill over direct heat for 1 hour turning once. Remove from grill.
• Venison or turkey burgers will not stick to grill when they are coated with nonstick cooking spray.
• For tender flavorful spareribs begin by parboiling them in pineapple juice. Then add a homemade barbecue sauce while grilling.
• Leftover barbecued pork chops make great sandwiches. Just remove meat from bones, reheat and serve on buns.
• Here's an easy marinade for grilled pork chops; for four chops, combine 1/2 cup each soy sauce, water and honey. Pour over chops and marinate, leave covered in the refrigerator overnight. Grill until done as desired.
• For fast, easy cleanup of food stuck inside pans, boil a little vinegar and water in the pan before washing. No scrubbing is required–the pan practically wipes clean.
• Instead of taking time to make meatballs make "meat squares". Spread meat mixture in jelly roll pan and bake over coals or in oven. Cut in small squares.
• To roast corn, pull back husks and remove silks. Replace husks and tie at top. Soak in salt water for 1 hour. Grill over hot coals for 15 to 20 minutes turning frequently.
• Presoak bamboo skewers in water for 20 minutes before threading with meat, veggies or fruit to prevent them from scorching or burning.
• Old baking pans (even garage sale finds) clean up easily after grilling if they are completely covered with aluminum foil first. Once the cooking is done just remove foil and discard.

• Store already made hamburger patties on tray between waxed paper. Can lift for accessibility once grilling starts.

BERRIES

• Using a potato blender is quicker than using a fork for mashing strawberries.
• Berries will keep up to a week refrigerated unwashed and unsweetened in a loosely covered container.
• When picking strawberries look under the leaves for the best berries as they will hide there.
• Thawed frozen berries will always be softer and juicier than fresh berries. Defrost the sealed bag of frozen berries in a larger bowl of cold water for 10 to 15 minutes, then use them in recipes where the extra juice is a bonus, such as over shortcake or in a sauce for pound cake.
• Strawberries can be used in punches as a garnish, in the ice ring itself, or as the base for a delicious punch. The berries can be mashed, strained to eliminate the seeds and doctored up as per recipe or imagination.
• Premeasure berries, rhubarb, etc. for future baking projects in amounts called for in favorite recipes. Prevents messy measuring later.
• Best way to pick berries is to pinch and twist the stems, leaving the hulls intact.
• Remove stem and hull from fresh strawberries with a tomato corer.
• Use sliced or mashed strawberries sprinkled with sugar for shortcake. If they stand for 20 to 30 minutes they will make their juice.
• Use whole strawberries with pointed ends facing upward if you plan to glaze recipe.
• Use egg slicer for cutting perfect slices of strawberries.

• Strawberries are best if picked red and firm, but may be ripened if left on counter for a day.
• For shortcake or scones use a rich hot fudge strawberry filling with one cup warmed hot topping and one cup sliced strawberries.

BREADS

• Always brush the tops of your yeast breads and rolls with melted butter when you put the dough into the pans, but do it before it raises a final time. Use just enough butter to glaze the top. This adds flavor and brown color. Brush tops again with soft butter.
• Add butterscotch chips to batter of pumpkin quick bread instead of raisins. More delicious!
• Shredded green tomatoes may be substituted for zucchini in a zucchini bread recipe.
• Homemade bread contains no preservatives and needs refrigeration.
• Bread that sounds hollow when tapped with fingers is baked perfectly.
• Dough rises better if kept out of drafts. Cover with towel and set over a pilot light on stove (if you have one). Let dough "rest" before rolling it out to shape it–it will be less elastic and easier to handle.
• Turn your basic recipe for 2 or 3 loaves of whole wheat bread into one for herb bread by adding 1/4 teaspoon each of marjoram, thyme, oregano and garlic powder and 1 tablespoon grated onion. Mix into the warm water or milk before adding the flour.
• For a crisp crust, brush the unbaked loaf with lightly beaten egg white. For a soft crust, brush the baked loaf with melted butter when it comes out of oven.
• Remove bread from pan to cool, so bottom will not stay moist.

• Bake quick breads one day before serving. Wrap and refrigerate. They have better texture and will slice better also.

• Don't overmix your batter when making quick bread or muffins. The finished product may crumble. Muffin batter should be lumpy.

• Brush Christmas yeast coffee cakes with lightly beaten egg white before baking. Then sprinkle with slivered almonds and white or colored sugar.

• Knead dough in a large resealable bag. Hands and countertops stay clean.

• When dissolving yeast, always remember to put about 1 teaspoon of sugar into lukewarm water or milk. It helps to get the dough working so yeast will raise. If yeast doesn't work you'll have a clump.

• For quick and easy garlic bread-sticks; split a hot dog bun down the middle and cut each 1/2 lengthwise. Butter each strip and sprinkle with garlic salt or powder. Place on baking sheet and broil until toasted.

• Put frozen bread loaves in a clean brown paper bag and place for 5 minutes in a 325° oven to thaw completely.

BREAKFAST

• Keep bacon slices from sticking together; heat a spatula over a burner, slide it under each slice to separate it from others.

• Use egg slicer to slice Kiwi uniformly.

• For a perfect fried egg, put a little butter, bacon grease, or side pork fat into a skillet (cast iron is best). If you want it sunny-side up, put a cover on and the steam will take care of the egg. if you want it over easy, flip the egg over, and count to five slowly. Leave it longer if you like the yolks hard.

• For crispy French toast, add a touch of cornstarch to the egg mixture.

• To butter many slices of bread quickly and evenly, heat the butter until soft. Then use a pastry brush to paint the butter on.

• For fluffier omelettes, add a pinch of cornstarch before beating.

• To ripen Kiwi's, place them in a brown paper bag with a banana or apple and leave at room temperature. When they are ready to eat, they should yield to slight pressure. Store ripe fruit in refrigerator for up to one week.

• To make an inexpensive syrup for pancakes, save small amounts of leftover jams and jellies in a jar. Or, fruit-flavored syrup can be made by adding 2 cups sugar to 1 cup of any kind of fruit juice and cooking until it boils.

• Freeze waffles that are left; they can be reheated in the toaster.

CAKES AND FROSTINGS

• When testing cake for doneness the rack may be pulled out a little only as it needs to stay close to the heat. Test with either toothpick or touch lightly with fingertips. If the cake bounces back it is done, if it leaves a dent, then it's not.

• To keep a cake from sliding on its plate during transit, drizzle a bit of frosting in a circle on the plate where the cake will rest before removing the cake from the pan. The frosting will hold the cake in place.

• Don't tamper with the mix or change it. If it says cream it means cream. If it says 2% then it means 2%.

• Sweeten whipped cream with confectioners' sugar instead of granulated sugar. It will stay fluffy and hold up a lot longer.

• Always refrigerate cream cheese-based frostings and fillings.

• Always let a cake cool 10 minutes before running a knife around the edge and turning out on a plate. An upside-down cake or jelly roll has to be removed at once.

• Spray measuring spoons or cups with a coating of nonstick cooking spray before measuring honey, syrup, or molasses. Sticky ingredients slide right out with no mess.

• If it calls for sour milk, and you have none, put 1 tablespoon of vinegar in one cup of milk, it will curdle immediately.

• Be sure your rack is in the center of the oven or the cake will come out too brown either on the top or bottom.

• If you are getting lopsided cakes then level up your stove.

• To prevent icing from running off your cake, try dusting the surface lightly with cornstarch before icing.

• If you forget to preheat the oven, turn the broiler on for a minute to get the temperature up fast.

• To dress up a plain frosted cake but have no sprinkles–crush sweetened cereal and scatter across the top. Adds a fun look and a nice crunch, too.

• When it says to grease pan, it means only the bottom as the cake has to have something to hold on to.

• To prepare muffins or cupcakes easily mix the batter in a pitcher so it can be poured in cups without making a mess.

• To improve an inexpensive cake mix, add one tablespoon of butter to the batter. This will make a richer-tasting cake.

• Try a little cream of tartar in your 7 minute icing, it will not get dry and cracked.

• Shortly before taking cupcakes from the oven, place a marshmallow on each for quick frosting.

• In place of flour use one teaspoon of tapioca for thickening in fruit pies.

COOKIES

• Flour the rolling pin slightly and roll lightly to desired thickness. Cut shapes close together and keep all trimmings for the last. Place pans in upper 1/3 of oven. Watch cookies carefully while baking to avoid burning edges.

• Use only stick butter or margarine in these recipes. Don't use reduced-fat or tub products. The fat and moisture content will yield poor results.

• For best results, bake one sheet of cookies at a time on the center rack of your oven. You can bake two sheets–halfway through baking, switch the pans from one rack to the other.

• Use outline (not solid) cookie cutters for napkins rings when having a party or country setting.

• Use electric knife to slice rolled-chilled cookie dough.

• For accuracy, measure liquids in clear measuring cups with spouts and hold the cup to eye level.

• Add 1/2 cup of sour cream to your peanut butter cookie recipe to make your cookies more moist.

• Most cookies can be stored at room temperature for a few days without losing flavor. For longer storage, place cookies and wax paper in layers in airtight container and freeze for 3 months.

• For chewy cookies, bake until edges are golden and the center looks slightly underbaked. Cool on baking sheets for 1 to 2 minutes before removing to a wire rack.

• When sprinkling sugar on cookies, try putting it into a salt shaker, as it saves time.

• Beat butter and sugar at medium speed. Beat dry ingredients at low speed. Don't overbeat. The dough should be just blended.

• Use nesting metal cups and spoons to measure flour and other dry ingredients. Before measuring, stir flour in its canister or package to aerate, then spoon it into appropriate-size measuring cup. Level off any excess with a metal spatula.

• Cookie dough that is to be rolled is much easier to handle after it has been in a cold place for 10 to 30 minutes. This keeps it from sticking, even though it may be soft. If not done, the dough may require more flour and too much flour makes the cookies hard and brittle. In rolling, take out on a floured board only as much dough as can be managed easily.

Lay a dampened cloth on your table or countertop before putting the cookie sheet down so it won't slide around while you fill it.

• Stale angel food cake can be cut into 1/2" slices and shaped with cookie cutters to make delicious "cookies". Just toast in the oven for a few minutes.

EGGS

• If you shake the egg and you hear a rattle, you can be sure it's stale. A really fresh egg will sink and a stale one will float.

• If you are making deviled eggs and want to slice it perfectly, dip the knife in water first. The slice will be smooth with no yolk sticking to the knife.

• The white of an egg is easiest to beat when it's at room temperature. So leave it out of the refrigerator about a half an hour before using it.

• To make light and fluffy scrambled eggs, add a little water while beating the eggs.

• Add vinegar to the water while boiling eggs. Vinegar helps to seal the egg, since it acts on the calcium in the shell.

• STORING EGGS: 1. Place your eggs in those tight-sealing egg containers and they will last longer in the refrigerator. You really shouldn't keep eggs longer than 11 days 2. Cover them with oil on the top in a sealed container in the refrigerator. 3. For long term storage: if there's a special on eggs at your local supermarket, you can take advantage of it. Just crack all the eggs open and put them in the freezer unit. To use one egg at a time, put single eggs in the ice tray. When frozen, put the egg cubes in a sealed plastic bag. You can take out the cubes one at a time for daily use. If you use eggs in twos or threes, freeze them that way in a plastic bag.

• To make quick-diced eggs, take your potato masher and go to work on a boiled egg.

• If you wrap each egg in aluminum foil before boiling it, the shell won't crack when it's boiling.

• To make those eggs go further when making scrambled eggs for a crowd, add a pinch of baking powder and 2 teaspoons of water per egg.

• A great trick for peeling eggs the easy way. When they are finished boiling, turn off the heat and just let them sit in the pan with the lid on for about 5 minutes. Steam will build up under the shell and they will just fall away.

• Or, quickly rinse hot hard-boiled eggs in cold water, and the shells will be easier to remove.

• Fresh or hard-boiled? Spin the egg. If it wobbles, it is raw - if it spins easily, it's hard boiled.

• Add a few drops of vinegar to the water when poaching an egg to keep it from running all over the pan.

• Add 1 tablespoon of water per egg white to increase the quantity of beaten egg white when making meringue.

• Fresh eggs are rough and chalky in appearance. Old eggs are smooth and shiny.

• Beaten egg whites will be more stable if you add 1 teaspoon cream of tartar to each cup of egg whites (7 or 8 eggs).

• Pierce the end of an egg with a pin, and it will not break when placed in boiling water.

• A small funnel is handy for separating egg whites from yolks. Open the egg over the funnel and the white will run through and the yolk will remain.

• For baking, it's best to use medium to large eggs. Extra large may cause cakes to fall when cooled.

• Brown and white shells are the same quantity.

• Egg whites can be kept up to 1 year. Add them to a plastic container as you "collect them" for use in meringues, angel food cake...1 cup equals 7 or 8 egg whites. You can also refreeze defrosted egg whites.

• For fluffier omelets, add a pinch of cornstarch before beating.

NUTS

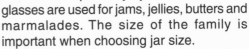

• Use English walnuts and Black Walnut extract as a substitute for Black Walnuts.

• Cut nut bars into festive shapes for fun and variety at Holiday time.

• Freeze nuts in shells a few days before cracking. The nutmeats will come out in larger pieces if they are frozen.

• Make holiday treat of 1 1/2 lbs. white, dark or milk chocolate and one can of mixed nuts. Drop teaspoonfuls onto waxed paper to harden. Store in airtight container.

• Before chopping nuts in a food processor, dust them with flour. This keeps the nuts from sticking to the processor.

• Toasted almonds will chop easier than untoasted ones.

• Shake chopped nuts in flour before adding to cake batter. This prevents them from sinking to the bottom.

• Use a blender for quick coarsely chopped almonds.

• Pecans stay fresh in refrigerator for 9 months and in freezer for 2 years.

• Wear rubber gloves when husking Black Walnuts to prevent stains to the hands.

• To quickly crack a large amount of nuts, put in a bag and gently hammer until they are cracked open. Then remove nutmeats with a pick.

• If nuts are stale, place them in the oven at 250°F and leave them there for 5 or 10 minutes. The heat will revive them.

PICKLING AND PRESERVING

• Quart jars are usually used for canning fruits, vegetables, meats and pickles. Pint jars are used for jams, preserves, relishes and sauces. Half-pint or jelly glasses are used for jams, jellies, butters and marmalades. The size of the family is important when choosing jar size.

• Pressure canning means to be done in a pressure cooker. Leave an inch space between jars after they have been taken out of the boiling water for air to circulate between the jars.

• Pickles and relishes can be eaten right away, but do get a better flavor the longer you wait. Dill pickles must wait 2 weeks.

• Use heavy stainless steel kettles when possible. Never cook vinegar in cheap aluminum as it will take on the taste.

• The number of jars you will get out of a recipe will vary because of the difference in the size and the moisture in the fruits and vegetables.

• For all canned pickles, relishes, and vegetables do not use iodized salt or the ingredients will get mushy.

• When filling jars always clean the tops off from spills.

• Syrups for jams and jellies will rise to top quickly and have to be watched very carefully.

• Spices may be added to pickles or relishes as are or may be tied up in a clean cloth, cooked with the pickles and discarded when cooking is done before jars are filled.

• Never sit hot jars in a draft.

• When they are cooling you will hear a popping if you are using the two-piece lids. That popping means that the jar has sealed. Press your finger on top; and if the cover is flat, it's okay. If jar has not sealed, use the contents–do not store.

• To scald your jars means to sterilize your empty jars by standing them upright in boiling water and filling with more boiling water and boil a minute or two.

• Sure-Jell helps set and speed-up jams and jellies but they can be cooked down low without it. Always ladle foam off of jams and jellies with a metal spoon.

PIES

• Insert a knife into the slits of a double-crusted pie, and it should come out clear. If it is sugary it needs more baking.

• Try not to make meringue on a humid day, since the sugar absorbs moisture and excess moisture may cause beading. Also be certain the sugar is completely dissolved during beating. Rub a small amount between your fingers-if it's grainy, continue to beat. Place the meringue over the hot filling. Keep filling warm while preparing meringue, pour it into the pie shell just before topping with meringue. Bake immediately at 350° for 15 minutes.

• Spread meringue so it extends out to the edge of the crust so it won't pull away. It's sealed.

• Add 1 or 2 tablespoons of molasses to pumpkin pie filling. It will make it richer in color and tastier, too.

• Use a thimble to cut holes in your top pie crusts. Then replace cut-out circles back in their holes. The hole will get bigger as pie bakes, giving an interesting pattern.

• If recipe calls for milk, use whole milk. Store-bought does not have as much butterfat as farm milk, but it is just fine.

• No matter how much salt a recipe calls for–put it in there as it is there for a reason.

• Make nice fat pies and heap the filling into the crusts.

• Place your pastry-lined pie plate on a partially pulled-out oven rack, then carefully fill with mixture. Gently push rack in stove.

• Place a piece of plastic wrap over cooked custard or pudding after pouring into pie shell to prevent a "skin" from forming.

• Add one tablespoon sesame seeds to pie crust recipe to have a tasty nutty flavor.

• Be sure your rolling pin is wood and heavy enough. Some are too light. A medium pin weighs about 5 lbs. and is fine.

• If a recipe calls for a cup, don't put in a rounded cup. Unless it says "heaping", use only a level measure.

• When measuring shortening for pie crust wet the cup first, and the shortening will slide right out.

• Where a recipe calls for 2 cups freshly whipped cream, use 12 ounces of Cool Whip.

SALADS

• Green peppers will not last long in the refrigerator. The best way to have them available is to freeze them. Wash them after hollowing out the insides, dry them and put them in a plastic bag. You can dice, strip, cube, or chip them.

• Iceberg lettuce as well as escarole and spinach is used for a bed for small and large salads, of any kind.

• The classic salad of iceberg lettuce is always welcome to the American table. It is used along with dressings or mixed with a variety of dark greens. It can be eaten dressed up very little or dressed up a lot with a variety of fruits, vegetables, meats, etc.

• Salads are light or complex and are usually chosen according to the meal they are served with. Fresh, tart greens will balance a heavy meal. A complex salad containing many ingredients will complement a lighter meal.

• Potato salads, a Waldorf salad, bean and mayo-dressed salads are generally informal, good picnic fare and healthy.

• Buffet salads are spreads with eye-appeal. They are molds, filled vegetable containers, marinated vegetables, and decoratively garnished salad platters.

• A basic earthy salad is nothing more than the edible parts of herbs and plants, gently seasoned with the most basic of spices or a sprinkling of lemon juice or vinegar and oil.

• Optimal freshness is the hallmark of a successful salad.

• Most salads should be served at room temperature.

• Flowers such as roses, daylillies, nasturtiums, geraniums and marigolds are commonly used in salads. They bruise easily so must be gotten early in the morning and handled carefully.

• Kale, beet greens, Swiss chard, bok choy, and the cabbages–including red, green and napa, and savory are all great additions to any salad, adding flavor and texture.

• To keep mint, lemon verbena, etc. from taking over your herb garden, pull your needed amounts by the roots. Enough root will remain for the plants to continue growing.

• Just about any cut of meat, fowl, or fish can be worked into a salad. Such salads can often be served as the main course. Remove all fat and gristle when preparing meat. Cut meat across the grain into even thickness strips. Arrange slices in a neat, decorative pattern on a platter.

• Place unripened tomatoes with other fruit, especially pears to speed up ripening.

• Commercial or homemade dressings are a matter of choice.

VEGETABLES

• To save potatoes before sprouting– peel, slice and boil them partially. Drain, cool and freeze. When needed pop frozen potatoes into boiling water, finish cooking and then mash.

• Use an egg slicer to slice mushrooms perfectly.

• Use an ice cream scoop to remove seeds from acorn or Hubbard squash or even pumpkin seeds from pumpkins.

• Freeze your onion surplus. Slice or dice and bake in a covered casserole at 350° until they're tender, about 20 to 30 minutes. Cool and pack them in freezer containers in recipe-sized portions. Freeze for up to 6 months. To use, thaw and warm with a little butter until light golden brown–perfect for casseroles, burgers or in gravies.

• When cutting corn from the cob to freeze, place end of cob in the hole of a Bundt pan. Cut corn off with sharp knife and corn will fall right in pan with little mess.

• One pound of fresh spinach will yield 10 to 12 cups of torn leaves; which will cook down to about one cup.

• Put foil under sweet potatoes before baking so sticky juices can't mess up oven.

• Bake a potato casserole right along with your roast.

• Use nylon stocking to dry onions. Put one in toe, tie a knot, put in onion, tie a knot-continue to stocking top. Hang in dry place. When needed cut one off between knots.

• Cook equal amounts of potatoes and turnips in boiling salted water until tender. Mash with milk and butter. Real treat!

• To preserve garden fresh carrots, dig from ground, wash well, dry overnight, pack in plastic bags and store in refrigerator and enjoy all winter.

• For a quick scalloped potato, combine frozen French fries with a homemade cheese sauce and bake until bubbly.

• Eating large cucumbers will cause chickens to produce eggs larger in size and amount.

• For the fluffiest mashed potatoes, use only russets and be careful not to overbeat. Cook just until tender; immediately drain and let stand uncovered for 1 to 2 minutes. While beating, slowly add warm milk. Do not add butter.

• If fresh vegetables are wilted or blemished, pick off the brown edges. Sprinkle with cool water, wrap in towel and refrigerate for an hour or so.

• Perk up soggy lettuce by adding lemon juice to a bowl of cold water and soak for an hour in the refrigerator.

• Lettuce and celery will crisp up fast if you place it in a pan of cold water and add a few sliced potatoes.

• If vegetables are overdone, put the pot in a pan of cold water. Let it stand from 15 minutes to 1/2 hour without scraping pan.

• By lining the crisper section of your refrigerator with newspaper and wrapping vegetables with it, moisture will be absorbed and your vegetables will stay fresher longer.

• Store leftover corn, peas, green beans, carrots, celery, potatoes and onions in a container in the freezer. Add to other ingredients when making stew.

• To keep the flavor in the vegetables, add a small amount of sugar to the water after cooking carrots, peas, beets, and corn.

• Substitute lemon pepper seasoning for table salt.

• Onions, broccoli and Brussels sprouts will cook faster if you make an X-shaped cut at the base of the vegetable.

• Overcooked potatoes can become soggy when the milk is added. Sprinkle with dry powdered milk for the fluffiest mashed potatoes ever.

• To hurry up baked potatoes, boil in salted water for 10 minutes, then place in a very hot oven. Or, cut potatoes in half and place them face down on a baking sheet in the oven to make the baking time shorter.

• Save some of the water in which the potatoes were boiled - add to some powdered milk and use when mashing. This restores some of the nutrients that were lost in the cooking process.

• Use a couple of tablespoons of cream cheese in place of butter for your potatoes; try using sour cream instead of milk when mashing.

• To avoid tears when peeling onions, peel them under cold water or refrigerate before chopping.

• For sandwiches to go in lunchboxes, sprinkle with dried onion. They will have turned into crisp pieces by lunchtime.

• Keep tomatoes in storage with stems pointed downward and they will retain their freshness longer.

• Sunlight doesn't ripen tomatoes. It's the warmth that makes them ripen. So find a warm spot near the stove or dishwasher where they can get a little heat.

• Save the juice from canned tomatoes in ice cube trays. When frozen, store in plastic bags in freezer for cooking use or for tomato drinks.

• Put vegetables in water after the water boils - not before - to be sure to preserve all the vegetables' vitamins.

• Squash that is leftover can be improved by adding some maple syrup before reheated.

• When cooking dried beans, add salt after cooking; if salt is added at the start, it will slow the cooking process.

• Adding sugar and horseradish to cooked carrots improves the flavor.

MISCELLANEOUS

Syrup: For each cup of light syrup in a recipe, substitute one cup of sugar and 1/4 cup water. For each cup of dark corn syrup, substitute 1 cup packed brown sugar and 1/4 cup water.

Treat for sauerkraut: To have a tangy combination add a can of whole-berry cranberry sauce to your package of sauerkraut as it's heating plus a little brown sugar. A real treat!

Frozen concentrate: To use frozen concentrate to prepare juice quickly, slide it into a pitcher, add some water and mash with a potato masher. Will be a lot quicker and dissolves readily.

Grated lemon peel: The quickest way to make grated lemon peel for recipes is to slice off big pieces of peel and grind them for just a few seconds in a food processor.

Hot chocolate: To prevent "skin" from forming on top of hot chocolate beverages, beat hot cocoa with whisk until foamy.

Stringing popcorn: If you plan to string popcorn, pop the popcorn a few days ahead. The kernels will not break as bad when needle is pushed through.

Ice water: Fill a clean plastic milk jug half full of water and freeze. When ice water is needed just finish filling with water and take along on a picnic, etc.

Brown sugar: A little brown sugar will help flavor chili.

Meatloaf: Put meatloaf ingredients in a bowl and mix with a potato masher to prevent a mess, especially on your hands.

Decorative potato or macaroni salad: For a decorative potato or macaroni salad, dissolve a little unflavored gelatin in a small amount of water and mix with the mayonnaise before adding to the salad. Spread the salad in a mold and chill. When turned out the salad will keep its shape.

Tender pancakes or waffles: For light and tender pancakes or waffles, separate the egg and beat the white until stiff. Stir the yolk and other liquid ingredients into the dry ingredients, then fold in the beaten egg white.

Venison: Cook venison in slow cooker. Add a tad of the apple pie spice and black pepper to cut the wild flavor.

Candles: Before having a party or decorating with candles, put candles in the freezer for a few hours. They will not drip wax then.

Salt: If stew is too salty, add raw cut potatoes and discard once they have cooked and absorbed the salt. Another remedy is to add a teaspoon each of cider vinegar and sugar. Or, simply add sugar.

If soup or stew is too sweet, add salt. For a main dish or vegetable, add a teaspoon of cider vinegar.

Gravy: To make gravy smooth, keep a jar with a mixture of equal parts of flour and cornstarch. Put 3 or 4 tablespoons of this mixture in another jar and add some water. Shake, and in a few minutes you will have a smooth paste for gravy.

To remedy greasy gravy, add a small amount of baking soda.

For quick thickener for gravies, add some instant potatoes to your gravy and it will thicken beautifully.

Pour a cup of brewed coffee around a roast or turkey as you put it in the oven. The dark savory gravy is always perfect.

Add a few teaspoons of soy sauce to gravies and stews for a great flavor and color.

Shrinkless links: Boil sausage links for about 8 minutes before frying and they will shrink less and not break at all. Or, you can roll them lightly in flour before frying.

A quick way to whip cream: A pinch of salt added to the cream before whipping strengthens the fat cells and makes them more elastic. This helps the cream stiffen much more quickly.

Cream that will not whip: Chill cream, bowl and beater well. Set bowl of cream into a bowl of ice water while you're whipping. Add the white of an egg. Chill and then whip. If the cream still does not stiffen, gradually whip in 3 or 4 drops of lemon juice. Cream whipped ahead of time will not separate if you add a touch of unflavored gelatin (1/4 teaspoon per cup of cream). To eliminate a lot of mess when whipping cream with an electric beater, try this: Cut 2 holes in the middle of a piece of waxed paper, then slip the stems of the beaters through the holes and attach the beaters to the machine. Simply place paper and beaters over the bowl and whip away.

Rock-hard brown sugar: Add a slice of soft bread to the package of brown sugar, close the bag tightly, and in a few hours the sugar will be soft again. If you need it in a hurry, simply grate the amount called for with a hand grater. Or, put brown sugar and a cup of water (do not add to the sugar, set it alongside of it) in a covered pan. Place in the oven (low heat) for a while. Or, buy liquid brown sugar.

Caked or clogged salt: Tightly wrap a piece of aluminum foil around the salt shaker. This will keep the dampness out of the salt. To prevent clogging, keep 5 to 10 grains of rice inside your shaker.

No spattering or sticking: To keep frying food from spattering, invert a metal colander over the pan, allowing steam to escape.

Always heat the frying pan before adding oil or butter. This will keep things from sticking to the pan.

Boil vinegar in a brand new frying pan to keep things from sticking to it.

Hurry-up hamburgers: Poke a hole in the middle of the patties while shaping them. The burgers will cook faster and the holes will disappear when done.

Removing the corn silk: Dampen a paper towel or terry cloth and brush downward on the cob of corn. Every strand should come off.

Preventing boil-overs: Add a lump of butter or a few teaspoons of cooking oil to the water. Rice, noodles or spaghetti will not boil over or stick together.

Softening butter: Soften butter quickly by grating it. Or heat a small pan and place it upside-down over the butter dish for several minutes. Or place in the microwave for a few seconds.

Measuring sticky liquids: Before measuring honey or syrup, oil the cup with cooking oil and rinse in hot water.

Scalded milk: Add a bit of sugar (without stirring) to milk to prevent it from scorching. Rinse the pan with cold water before scalding milk, and it will be much easier to clean.

Tenderized meat: Boiled meat: Add a tablespoon of vinegar to the cooking water. Tough meat or game: Make a marinade of equal parts cooking vinegar and heated bouillon. Marinate for 2 hours. Steak: Simply rub in a mixture of cooking vinegar and oil. Allow to stand for 2 hours. Chicken: To stew an old hen, soak it in vinegar for several hours before cooking. It will taste like a spring chicken.

Unpleasant cooking odors: While cooking vegetables that give off unpleasant odors, simmer a small pan of vinegar on top of the stove. Or, add vinegar to the cooking water. To remove the odor of fish from cooking and serving implements, rinse in vinegar water.

Clean and deodorize your cutting board: Bleach it clean with lemon juice. Take away strong odors like onion with baking soda. Just rub it in.

Keep the color in beets: If you find that your beets tend to lose color when you boil them, add a little lemon juice.

No-smell cabbage: Two things to do to keep cabbage smell from filling the kitchen: don't overcook it (keep it crisp) and put half a lemon in the water when you boil it.

A great energy saver: When you're near the end of the baking time, turn the oven off and keep the door closed. The heat will stay the same long enough to finish baking your cake or pie and you'll save all that energy.

Special looking pies: Give a unique look to your pies by using pinking shears to cut the dough. Make a pinked lattice crust!

Removing ham rind: Before placing ham in the roasting pan, slit rind lengthwise on the underside. The rind will peel away as the ham cooks, and can be easily removed.

Unmolding gelatin: Rinse the mold pan in cold water and coat with salad oil. The oil will give the gelatin a nice luster and it will easily fall out of the mold.

No-spill cupcakes: An ice cream scoop can be used to fill cupcake papers without spilling.

Slicing cake or torte: Use dental floss to slice evenly and cleanly through a cake or torte - simply stretch a length of the floss taut and press down through the cake.

Ice cream: Buy bulk quantities of ice cream and pack in small margarine containers. These provide individual servings.

Canning peaches: Don't bother to remove skins when canning or freezing peaches. They will taste better and be more nutritious with the skin on.

How to chop garlic: Chop in a small amount of salt to prevent pieces from sticking to the knife or chopped board. Then pulverize with the tip of the knife.

Excess fat on soups or stews: Remove fat from stews or soups by refrigerating and eliminating fat as it rises and hardens on the surface. Or add lettuce leaves to the pot - the fat will cling to them. Discard lettuce before serving.

Broiled meat drippings: Place a piece of bread under the rack on which you are broiling meat. Not only will this absorb the dripping fat, but it will reduce the chance of the fat catching on fire.

Fake sour cream: To cut down on calories, run cottage cheese through the blender. It can be flavored with chives, extracts, etc., and used in place of mayonnaise.

Browned butter: Browning brings out the flavor of the butter, so only half as much is needed for seasoning vegetables if it is browned before it is added.

Fresh garlic: Peel garlic and store in a covered jar of vegetable oil. The garlic will stay fresh and the oil will be nicely flavored for salad dressings.

Fluffy rice: Rice will be fluffier and whiter if you add 1 teaspoon of lemon juice to each quart of water.

Nutritious rice: Cook rice in liquid saved from cooking vegetables to add flavor and nutrition. A nutty taste can be achieved by adding wheat germ to the rice.

Jar labels: Attach canning labels to the lids instead of the sides of jelly jars, to prevent the chore of removing the labels when the contents are gone.

Flour puff: Keep a powder puff in your flour container to easily dust your rolling pin or pastry board.

Perfect noodles: When cooking noodles, bring required amount of water to a boil, add noodles, turn heat off and allow to stand for 20 minutes. This prevents overboiling and the chore of stirring. Noodles won't stick to the pan with this method.

Easy croutons: Make delicious croutons for soup or salad by saving toast, cutting into cubes, and sautéing in garlic butter.

Baked fish: To keep fish from sticking to the pan, bake on a bed of chopped onion, celery and parsley. This also adds a nice flavor to the fish.

Non-sticking bacon: Roll a package of bacon into a tube before opening. This will loosen the slices and keep them from sticking together.

Tasty hot dogs: Boil hot dogs in sweet pickle juice and a little water for a different taste.

Grating cheese: Chill the cheese before grating and it will take much less time.

Golden-brown chicken: For golden-brown fried chicken, roll it in powdered milk instead of flour.

Double boiler hint: Toss a few marbles in the bottom of a double boiler. When the water boils down the noise will let you know!

Different meatballs: Try using crushed cornflakes or corn bread instead of bread crumbs in a meatball recipe. Or use onion-flavored potato chips.

CLEAN-UP TIPS

Appliances: To shine chrome, use vinegar or window cleaner.

If the numbers on your oven dial are worn, take a yellow crayon and rub it all over the number on the dial. Gently wipe off the excess crayon and paint with the clear nail polish.

To clean splattered food from the interior of your microwave, bring one cup of water to a boil until steam forms on the inside walls of microwave. Remove water and wipe with a damp cloth. You may have to repeat the process to get a really big job done.

To rid yellowing from white appliances try this: Mix together: 1/2 cup bleach, 1/4 cup baking soda and 4 cups warm water. Apply with a sponge and let set for 10 minutes. Rinse and dry thoroughly.

Instead of using commercial waxes, shine with rubbing alcohol.

For quick clean-ups, rub with equal parts of water and household ammonia.

Or, try club soda. It cleans and polishes at the same time.

Blender: Fill part way with hot water and add a drop of detergent. Cover and turn it on for a few seconds. Rinse and drain dry.

Copper pots: Fill a spray bottle with vinegar and add 3 tablespoons of salt. Spray solution liberally on copper pot. Let set for a while, then simply rub clean.

Dip lemon halves in salt and rub.

Or, rub with Worcestershire sauce or catsup. The tarnish will disappear.

Clean with toothpaste and rinse.

Burnt and scorched pans: Sprinkle burnt pans liberally with baking soda, adding just enough water to moisten. Let stand for several hours. You can generally lift the burned portions right out of the pan.

Stubborn stains on non-stick cookware can be removed by boiling 2 tablespoons of baking soda, 1/2 cup vinegar and 1 cup water for 10 minutes. Re-season pan with salad oil.

Cast-iron skillets: Clean the outside of the pan with commercial oven cleaner. Let set for 2 hours and the accumulated black stains can be removed with vinegar and water.

Can opener: Loosen grime by brushing with an old toothbrush. To thoroughly clean blades, run a paper towel through the cutting process.

Enamelware or casserole dishes: Fill a dish that contains stuck food bits with boiling water and 2 tablespoons of baking soda. Let it stand and wash out.

Dishes: Save time and money by using the cheapest brand of dishwashing detergent available, but add a few tablespoons of vinegar to the dishwater. The vinegar will cut the grease and leave your dishes sparkling clean.

Before washing fine china and crystal, place a towel on the bottom of the sink to act as a cushion.

To remove coffee or tea stains and cigarette burns from fine china. Rub with a damp cloth dipped in baking soda.

Dishwasher: Run a cup of white vinegar through the entire cycle in an empty dishwasher to remove all soap film.

Clogged drains: When a drain is clogged with grease, pour a cup of salt and a cup of baking soda into the drain followed by a kettle of boiling water. The grease will usually dissolve immediately and open the drain.

Coffee grounds are a no-no. They do a nice job of clogging, especially if they get mixed with grease.

Curtains: To freshen curtains, throw in the dryer with a fabric softener sheet and a damp towel.

Cobwebs: To remove cobwebs, clean with an upward motion to lift them off. Downward motions tend to splatter them against walls.

Dusting: Spray furniture polish on the bristles of your broom and the dust and dirt will be easier to collect when you sweep.

Dish Drainer: Remove hard water stains from your dish drainer by tilting the low end of the board slightly and pouring one cup of white vinegar over the board. Let it set overnight and rub off with a sponge in the morning.

Garbage disposal: Grind a half lemon or orange rind in the disposal to remove any unpleasant odor.

Glassware: Never put a delicate glass in hot water bottom side first; it will crack from sudden expansion. The most delicate glassware will be safe if it is slipped in edgewise.

Vinegar is a must when washing crystal. Rinse in 1 part vinegar to 3 parts warm water. Air dry.

When one glass is tucked inside another, do not force them apart. Fill the top glass with cold water and dip the lower one in hot water. They will come apart without breaking.

Grater: For a fast and simple clean-up, rub salad oil on the grater before using.

Use a toothbrush to brush lemon rind, cheese, onion or whatever out of the grater before washing it.

Meat Grinder: Before washing, run a piece of bread through it.

Oven: Following a spill, sprinkle with salt immediately. When oven is cool, brush off burnt food and wipe with a damp sponge.

Sprinkle bottom of oven with automatic dishwasher soap and cover with wet paper towels. Let stand for a few hours.

A quick way to clean oven parts is to place a bath towel in the bathtub and pile all removable parts from the oven onto it. Draw enough hot water to just cover the parts and sprinkle a cup of dishwasher soap over it. While you are cleaning the inside of the oven, the rest will be cleaning itself.

An inexpensive oven cleaner: Set oven on warm for about 20 minutes, then turn off. Place a small dish of full strength ammonia on the top shelf. Put a large pan of boiling water on the bottom shelf and let it set overnight. In the morning, open oven and let it air a while before washing off with soap and water. Even the hard baked-on grease will wash off easily.

Plastic cups, dishes and containers: Coffee or tea stains can be scoured with baking soda.

Or, fill the stained cup with hot water and drop in a few denture cleanser tablets. Let soak for 1 hour.

To rid foul odors from plastic containers, place crumpled-up newspaper (black and white only) into the container. Cover tightly and leave overnight.

Refrigerator: To help eliminate odors fill a small bowl with charcoal (the kind used for potted plants) and place it on a shelf in the refrigerator. It absorbs odors rapidly.

An open box of baking soda will absorb food odors for at least a month or two.

A little vanilla poured on a piece of cotton and placed in the refrigerator will eliminate odors.

To prevent mildew from forming, wipe with vinegar. The acid effectively kills the mildew fungus.

Use a glycerine soaked cloth to wipe sides and shelves. Future spills wipe up easily. And after the freezer has been defrosted, coat the inside coils with glycerin. The next time you defrost, the ice will loosen quickly and drop off in sheets.

Wash inside and out with a mixture of 3 tablespoons of baking soda in a quart of warm water.

Sinks: For a sparkling white sink, place paper towels across the bottom of your sink and saturate with household bleach. Let set for 1/2 hour or so.

Rub stainless steel sinks with lighter fluid if rust marks appear. After the rust disappears wipe with your regular kitchen cleanser.

Use a cloth dampened with rubbing alcohol to remove water spots from stainless steel. Spots on stainless steel can also be removed with white vinegar.

Club soda will shine up stainless steel sinks in a jiffy.

Teakettle: To remove lime deposits, fill with equal parts of vinegar and water. Bring to a boil and allow to stand overnight.

Thermos bottle: Fill the bottle with warm water, add 1 teaspoon of baking soda and allow to soak.

Tin pie pans: Remove rust by dipping a raw potato in cleaning powder and scouring.

To unplug sink: Pour in one cup or more of white vinegar and a cup of baking soda, then add hot water out of the tap at full force. When bubbling stops, drain should be clear. Need no plumber.

Fingerprints off the kitchen door and walls: Take away fingerprints and grime with a solution of half water and half ammonia. Put in a spray bottle from one of these expensive cleaning products, you'll never have to buy them again.

Formica tops: Polish them to a sparkle with club soda.

Silver: Clean with toothbrush.

WINDOWS

Window cleaning: Newspaper is much cheaper to use for drying freshly-washed windows than paper toweling.

Drying windows: Dry the inside panes with up-and-down strokes, and the outside with back-and-forth motions to see which side has smudges.

Window cleaning solution: The best mixture for cleaning windows is 1/2 cup of ammonia, 1 cup of white vinegar and 2 tablespoons of cornstarch in a bucket of warm water.

Cold weather window cleaning: Add 1/2 cup of rubbing alcohol to the above mixture on cold days to prevent ice from forming on your windows.

Clean window sills: To remove spots on window sills, rub the surface with rubbing alcohol.

Aluminum window frames: Use cream silver polish to clean aluminum window frames.

Grease spots: Any cola drink will remove grease spots from windows.

Numbered windows: When cleaning, painting or changing windows, number each with a ballpoint pen and put the corresponding number inside the proper window frame.

Window shade tears: Repair with colorless nail polish. This works wonders on small tears.

Cleaning screens: For a thorough job, brush on both sides with kerosene. Wipe with a clean cloth. This method will also prevent rust from forming. Be sure to dust the screens with a small paintbrush before you begin.

For small jobs, rub a brush-type hair roller lightly over the screen and see how easily it picks up all the lint and dust.

FURNITURE

To remove polish build-up: Mix 1/2 cup vinegar and 1/2 cup water. Rub with a soft cloth that has been moistened with solution, but wrung out. Dry immediately with another soft cloth.

Polishing carved furniture: Dip an old soft toothbrush into furniture polish and brush lightly.

Cigarette burns: For small minor burns, try rubbing mayonnaise into the burn. Let set for a while before wiping off with a soft cloth. Burns can be repaired with a wax stick (available in all colors at paint and hardware stores). Gently scrape away the charred finish. Heat a knife blade and melt the shellac stick against the heated blade. Smooth over damaged area with your finger. But always consider the value of the furniture. It might be better to have a professional make the repair.

Or, make a paste of rottenstone (available at hardware stores) and salad oil. Rub into the burned spot only, following the grain of wood. Wipe clean with a cloth that has been dampened in oil. Wipe dry and apply your favorite furniture polish.

Scratches: Make sure you always rub with the grain of the wood when repairing a scratch. Walnut: Remove the meat from a fresh, unsalted walnut or pecan nut. Break it in half and rub the scratch with the broken side of the nut.

Mahogany: You can either rub the scratch with a dark brown crayon or buff with brown paste wax.

Red Mahogany: Apply ordinary iodine with a number O artist's brush.

Maple: Combine equal amounts of iodine and denatured alcohol. Apply with a Q-tip, then dry, wax and buff.

Ebony: Use black shoe polish, black eyebrow pencil or black crayon.

Teakwood: Rub very gently with 0000 steel wool. Rub in equal amounts of linseed oil and turpentine.

Light-finished furniture: Scratches can be hidden by using tan shoe polish. However, only on shiny finishes.

For all minor scratches: Cover each scratch with a generous amount of white petroleum jelly. Allow it to remain on for 24 hours. Rub into wood. Remove excess and polish as usual.

For larger scratchers: Fill by rubbing with a wax stick (available in all colors at your hardware or paint store) or a crayon that matches the finish of the wood.

Removing paper that is stuck to a wood surface: Do not scrape with a knife. Pour any salad oil, a few drops at a time, on the paper. Let set for a while and rub with a soft cloth. Repeat the procedure until the paper is completely gone.

Old decals can be removed easily by painting them with several coats of white vinegar. Give the vinegar time to soak in, then gently scrape off.

Three solutions to remove white water rings and spots: Dampen a soft cloth with water and put a dab of toothpaste on it. For stubborn stains, add baking soda to the toothpaste.

Make a paste of butter or mayonnaise and cigarette ashes. Apply to spot and buff away. Apply a paste of salad oil and salt. Let stand briefly. Wipe and polish.

Marble table-top stains: Sprinkle salt on a fresh-cut lemon. Rub very lightly over stain. Do not rub hard or you will ruin the polished surface. Wash off with soap and water.

Scour with a water and baking soda paste. Let stand for a few minutes before rinsing with warm water.

Removing candle wax from wooden finishes: Soften the wax with a hair dryer. Remove wax with paper toweling and wash down with a solution of vinegar and water.

Plastic table tops: You will find that a coat of Turtle Wax is a quick pick-up for dulled plastic table tops and counters.
Or, rub in toothpaste and buff.

Glass table tops: Rub in a little lemon juice. Dry with paper towels and shine with newspaper for a sparkling table.
Toothpaste will remove small scratches from glass.

Chrome cleaning: For sparkling clean chrome without streaks, use a cloth dampened in ammonia.

Removing glue: Cement glue can be removed by rubbing with cold cream, peanut butter or salad oil.

Wicker: Wicker needs moisture, so use a humidifier in the winter.
To prevent drying out, apply lemon oil occasionally.
Never let wicker freeze. This will cause cracking and splitting.
Wash with a solution of warm salt water to keep from turning yellow.

Metal furniture: To remove rust, a good scrubbing with turpentine should accomplish this job.

Vinyl upholstery: Never oil vinyl as this will make it hard. It is almost impossible to soften again. For proper cleaning, sprinkle baking soda or vinegar on a rough, damp cloth, then wash with a mild dishwashing soap.

Leather upholstery: Prevent leather from cracking by polishing regularly with a cream made of 1 part vinegar and 2 parts linseed oil. Clean with a damp cloth and saddle soap.

Grease stains: Absorb grease on furniture by pouring salt on the spill immediately.

Soiled upholstery: Rub soiled cotton upholstery fabric with an artgum eraser or squares (purchased at stationery store).

LAUNDRY

Spot removal: Two parts water and one part rubbing alcohol are the basic ingredients in any commercial spot remover.

Clean machine: Fill your washer with warm water and add a gallon of distilled vinegar. Run the machine through the entire cycle to unclog and clean soap scum from hoses.

Too sudsy: When your washer overflows with too many suds, sprinkle salt in the water - the suds will disappear.

Hand-washed sweaters: Add a capful of hair cream rinse to the final rinse water when washing sweaters.

Whiter fabric: Linen or cotton can be whitened by boiling in a mixture or 1 part cream of tartar and 3 parts water.

Whitest socks: Boil socks in water to which a lemon slice has been added.

Freshen feather pillows: Put feather pillows in the dryer and tumble, then air outside.

Lintless corduroy: While corduroy is still damp, brush with clothes brush to remove all lint.

Ironing tip: When pressing pants, iron the top part on the wrong side. Iron the legs on the right side. This gives the pockets and waistband a smooth look.

Creaseless garments: Take an empty cardboard paper towel roll and cut through it lengthwise. Slip it over a wire hanger to prevent a crease from forming in the garment to be hung on the hanger.

Remove creases from hems: Sponge material with a white vinegar solution and press flat to remove creases in hems.

Bedroom ironing: A good place to iron is in the bedroom. Closets are nearby to hang clothes up immediately, and the bed makes a good surface on which to fold clothes and separate items into piles.

Ironing board cover: When washing your ironing board cover, attach it to the board while it is still damp. When it dries, the surface will be completely smooth.

Starch your ironing board cover. This helps the cover stay clean longer.

Lint remover: Add a yard of nylon netting to your dryer with the wet clothes - it will catch most of the lint.

Washer advice: Button all buttons on clothing and turn inside out before putting into the washer. Fewer buttons will fall off and garments will fade less if turned inside out.

Soiled collars: Use a small paintbrush and brush hair shampoo into soiled shirt collars before laundering. Shampoo is made to dissolve body oils.

Faster ironing: Place a strip of heavy-duty aluminum foil over the entire length of the ironing board and cover with pad. As you iron, heat will reflect through the underside of the garment.

Ironing embroidery: Lay the embroidery piece upside-down on a Turkish towel before ironing. All the little spaces between the embroidery will be smooth when you are finished.

BATHROOM

Bathroom tile: Rub ordinary car wax into your ceramic bathroom tiling to clean and refinish. Let it stand 10 minutes and buff or polish.

Use a typewriter eraser to clean spaces between bathroom tiles.

Ceramic tiles

Before cleaning bathroom tiles, run the shower on *Hot* for 5 minutes to steam the dirt loose.

Metal shower head: To clean mineral deposits from a clogged shower head, boil it with half a cup of white vinegar.

Plastic shower head: Soak a plastic shower head in a hot vinegar and water mixture to unclog it.

Shower curtains: Before hanging shower curtains, soak them in a salt water solution to prevent mildew.

To remove mildew on shower curtains, wash them in hot soapy water, rub with lemon juice, and let them dry in the sun.

Bathroom fixtures: Dip a cloth in kerosene or rubbing alcohol to remove scum from your bathroom fixtures.

Removing film and scum: Use a piece of very fine steel wool to remove film from the shower stall.

Porcelain cleaners: Lighter fluid will remove most dark, stubborn stains from sink and bathtub.

Easy bathroom cleaning: Clean your bathroom after a steamy bath or shower. The walls, fixtures, etc., will be much easier to clean because the steam will have loosened the dirt.

Yellowed bathtub: Restore whiteness to a yellowed bathtub by rubbing with a salt and turpentine solution.

Toilet: Sometimes moisture accumulates around the toilet, leaving puddles on the floor. Prevent the condensation by applying a coat of floor wax to the tank.

Rust stains: Spread a paste of hydrogen peroxide and cream of tartar over the area, and add a few drops of ammonia. Let it stand for 2 or 3 hours.

Medicine cabinet: It's a good idea to go through your medicine cabinet several times a year and throw away medicines that are old or outdated. They could be dangerous.

Cleaning shower doors: Rub glass shower doors with a white vinegar-dampened sponge to remove soap residue.

Steam-free mirror: If your medicine cabinet has two sliding mirrors, slide one side open before taking a bath or shower. After the bath, you'll have one clean mirror instead of two that are steamed and foggy.

Steamy bathrooms: If you run about an inch of cold water before adding hot water to your bath, there will be absolutely no steam in your bathroom.

Rusty tile: Rust stains on tile can be removed with kerosene.

Sink cleaners: Light stains can often be removed by simply rubbing with a cut lemon. For dark stains, and especially rust, rub with a paste of borax and lemon juice.

Sweet-smelling bathroom: Place a fabric softener sheet in the wastepaper basket. Or, add a touch of fragrance by dabbing your favorite perfume on a light bulb. When the light is on, the heat releases the aroma.

HANDY PERSON

Plywood cutting: Put a strip of masking tape at the point of plywood where you plan to begin sawing to keep it from splitting.

Locating wall studs: Move a pocket compass along the wall. When the needle moves, usually the stud will be located at that point. Studs are usually located 16" apart.

Fraying rope: Shellac the ends of the rope to prevent fraying.

Heat the cut end of the nylon cord over a match flame to bond the end together.

Loosening rusty bolts: Apply a cloth soaked in any carbonated soda to loosen rusted bolts.

Sandpaper hint: By dampening the backing on sandpaper, it will last longer and resist cracking.

Tight screws: Loosen a screw by putting a couple of drops of peroxide on it and letting it soak in.

Loose drawer knobs: Before inserting a screw into the knob, coat with fingernail polish to hold it tightly.

Screwdriver tip: Keep a screwdriver tip from slipping by putting chalk on the blade.

Loosening joints: Loosen old glue by applying vinegar from an oil can to the joint.

Rule to remember: Left is loose and right is tight.

Sticking drawers: Rub the runners of drawers with a candle or a bar of soap so they will slide easily.

Stubborn locks: Dip key into machine oil or graphite to loosen up a lock.

Slamming doors: Reduce the noise level in your home by putting self-sticking protective pads on the inside edges of cabinet doors, cupboards, etc.

Icy sidewalk tip: Sprinkle sand through a strainer on an icy sidewalk to distribute evenly.

Garbage can tip: Garbage cans will last longer if they are painted. Use primer on galvanized metal, then paint with matching house paint.

Towel rack tip: Replace the bottom screws of towel racks with cup hooks. Small towels and washcloths may be hung from them.

Screen repair: Use clear cement glue to repair a small hole in wire screening.

Hairdryer hint: Thaw a frozen pipe with a portable hairdryer.

Finding a gas leak: Lather the pipes with soapy water. The escaping gas will cause the soapy water to bubble, revealing the damaged areas. You can make a temporary plug by moistening a cake of soap and pressing it over the spot. When the soap hardens, it will effectively close the leak until the gasman comes.

Hanging pictures: Before you drive nails into the wall, mark the spot with an X of cellophane tape. This trick will keep the plaster from cracking when you start hammering.

When the landlady says, "no nails in the wall", hang pictures with sewing machine needles. They will hold up to 30 pounds.

BEAUTY

Natural facial: A good and inexpensive facial to try; mash half an avocado, spread thickly on face and remove with warm water 20 minutes later.

Sunburn relief: A wonderful relief for sunburn pain is the application of mint-flavored milk of magnesia to the skin.

Dab on some apple cider vinegar. The pinkness and pain will disappear.

For a super bad burn, put on a paste of water and baking soda.

Hair shiner: These hair rinses will remove soap film and shine hair: For blondes, rinse water containing a few tablespoons of lemon juice. For brunettes and redheads, a few tablespoons of apple cider vinegar in the rinse water.

Broken lipstick: Hold a match under the broken ends until they melt enough to adhere to each other. Cool in the refrigerator.

Nail polish: Don't throw away that gummy nail polish. Place the bottle in boiling water to bring it back to its original consistency.

Instead of storing the nail polish bottle right-side-up, put it on its side. Stir it up with the brush when you need some.

Before you put on polish, put vinegar on your nails. It will clean them completely and help nail polish stick longer.

Your own manicure: Soak your hands in warm water with lemon juice added. Take them out after about 8 minutes. Rub some lemon peel over the nails while you gently push back the cuticle. Then buff with a soft cloth.

Baking soda for teeth: Baking soda instead of toothpaste does as good a job. It also works on dentures.

Cleaning combs and brushes: A solution of baking soda and hot water cleans hair brushes and combs.

Hair conditioner: Mayonnaise gives dry hair a good conditioning. Apply 1/2 cup mayonnaise to dry, unwashed hair. Cover with plastic bag and wait for 15 minutes. Rinse a few times before shampooing thoroughly.

Tired eyes: Place fresh cold cucumbers slices on your eyelids to rid them of redness and puffiness.

Dry skin: The best remedy is also the easiest to find: water. Drink six to eight glasses a day and eat foods high in water content, such as fruits and leafy vegetables. Use a humidifier in winter.

Bathe in mildly salted water (1/2 cup of salt per bath) to rehydrate your body, then apply a cream or lotion that will act as a moisturizer.

For an easy facial, mash a banana, add a tablespoon of honey and smooth the mixture on your face. After 15 minutes, rinse with warm water.

Oily skin: To help normalize skin, avoid spicy foods, reduce oils and fats in your diet and drink six to eight glasses of water daily. For a refreshing facial, fill a spray bottle with tepid water and 1 teaspoon of salt, then spray the solution on your face. Blot dry with a towel. For a quick steam, heat a wet towel in the microwave and form a tent over your face.

Here's a quick facial mask: Mix 3 tablespoons each of mineral water and Fuller's Earth and apply the paste to your face. After 20 minutes rinse with warm water. Or try a paste of warm water and oatmeal for 10 minutes.

Pimples: Here's some single-pimple camouflage: use a little green eye shadow to neutralize the redness, then cover with foundation.

Puffiness: If your hands are puffy, hold them over your head for a couple of minutes; repeat at least three or four times a day. Elevate swollen feet for a minimum of 15 minutes.

SEWING

Threading needles: Apply some hair spray to your finger and to the end of the thread, stiffening it enough to be easily threaded.

Sharp machine needles: Sharpen sewing machine needles by stitching through sandpaper.

Buttons: Coat the center of buttons with clear nail polish and they'll stay on longer. On a four-hole button, sew through two holes at a time, knotting the thread and tying off for each set of holes.

Use dental floss or elastic thread to sew buttons on children's clothing. The buttons will take a lot of wear before falling off.

Dropped needles and pins: Instead of groping around your floor for fallen needles and pins, keep a magnet in your sewing kit, simply sweep it across your rug to pick up those strays.

Sewing machine oil: Stitch through a blotter after oiling your sewing machine to prevent extra oil from damaging your garments.

Patterns: Instead of trying to fit used patterns back into their envelopes, store them in plastic bags.

Keep patterns from tearing and wrinklefree by spraying with spray starch.

Heavy seams: Rub seams with a bar of soap to allow a sewing machine needle to easily pass through.

Sewing on nylon: When repairing seams on nylon jackets or lingerie, make the job a lot simpler by placing a piece of paper underneath the section you are going to sew. Stitch through the fabric and paper. When finished, tear the paper off.

FOOD STORAGE

Baking Powder: Store the airtight tins in a cool, dry place and replace every 6 months.

Baking Soda: Store in an airtight container in a cool, dry place for about 6 months.

Beans: Once a package is opened, dry beans should not be refrigerated but stored in airtight containers in a cold, dry place. They will keep for about 1 year.

Bread: A rib of celery in your bread bag will keep the bread fresh for a longer time.

Brown Sugar: Wrap in a plastic bag and store in a tightly covered container for up to 4 months.

Cakes: Putting half an apple in the cake box will keep cake moist.

Celery and lettuce: Store in refrigerator in paper bags instead of plastic. Leave the outside leaves and stalks on until ready to use.

Cheese: Wrap cheese in a vinegar-dampened cloth to keep it from drying out.

Chocolate: Store chocolate for no longer than 1 year. It should be kept in a cool, dry place with a temperature range of 60°F to 75°F. If the storage temperature exceeds 75°F, some of the cocoa butter may separate and rise to the surface, causing a whitish color to the chocolate called "bloom".

Cocoa: Store cocoa in a glass jar in a dry and cool place.

Cookies: Place crushed tissue paper on the bottom of your cookie jar.

Cottage Cheese: Store carton upside-down. It will keep twice as long.

Dried Fruit: Store unopened packages of dried fruit in a cool, dry place or in the refrigerator. Store opened packages in an airtight container in the refrigerator or freezer for 6 to 8 months.

Flour: Store flour in a clean, tightly covered container for up to 1 year at room temperature.

Garlic: Garlic should be stored in a dry, airy place away from light. Garlic cloves can be kept in the freezer. When ready to use, peel and chop before thawing. Or, garlic cloves will never dry out if you store them in a bottle of cooking oil. After the garlic is used up, you can use the garlic flavored oil for salad dressing.

Granulated Sugar: Store sugar in a tightly covered container for up to 2 years.

Honey: Put honey in small plastic freezer containers to prevent sugaring. It also thaws out in a short time.

Ice Cream: Ice cream that has been opened and returned to the freezer sometimes forms a waxlike film on the top. To prevent this, after part of the ice cream has been removed press a piece of waxed paper against the surface and reseal the carton.

Lemons: Store whole lemons in a tightly sealed jar of water in the refrigerator. They will yield much more juice than when first purchased.

Limes: Store limes, wrapped in tissue paper, on lower shelf of the refrigerator.

Marshmallows: They will not dry out if stored in the freezer. Simply cut with scissors when ready to use.

Nuts: For optimum freshness and shelf life, nuts should be stored, preferably unshelled, in a tightly covered container in the refrigerator or freezer and shelled as needed. (The shell and the cool temperature keep the nut from turning rancid.)

Olive Oil: You can lengthen the life of olive oil by adding a cube of sugar to the bottle.

Onions: Wrap individually in foil to keep them from becoming soft or sprouting. Once an onion has been cut in half, rub the leftover side with butter and it will keep fresh longer.

Parsley: Keep fresh and crisp by storing in a wide-mouth jar with a tight lid. Parsley may also be frozen.

Popcorn: It should always be kept in the freezer. Not only will it stay fresh, but freezing helps eliminate "old-maids".

Potatoes: Potatoes, as well as other root vegetables, keep well in a dark, cool place,

preferably a cellar. Store them in a dark brown paper bag.

Shredded Coconut: Store in a cool, dry place in an airtight container. Do not store in the refrigerator.

Smoked Meats: Wrap ham or bacon in a vinegar-soaked cloth, then in waxed paper to preserve freshness.

Soda Crackers: Wrap tightly and store in the refrigerator.

Strawberries: Keep in a colander in the refrigerator. Wash just before serving.

Vegetables with tops: Remove the tops on carrots, beets, etc. before storing.

Yeast: Store in the freezer or refrigerator in a closed plastic bag.

MEAT

Beef

Roasts	3 to 5 days
Steaks	3 to 5 days
Ground beef, stew meat	2 days

Pork

Roasts	3 to 5 days
Hams, picnics, whole	7 days
Bacon	7 to 14 days
Chops, spareribs	2 to 3 days
Pork sausage	1 to 2 days

Veal

Roasts	3 to 5 days
Chops	4 days

Lamb

Roasts	3 to 5 days
Chops	3 to 5 days
Ground lamb	2 days

Poultry

Chickens, whole	1 to 2 days
Chickens, cut up	2 days
Turkeys, whole	1 to 2 days

Cooked meats

Leftover cooked meats	4 days
Cooked poultry	2 days
Hams, picnics	7 days
Frankfurters	4 to 5 days
Sliced luncheon meats	3 days
Unsliced bologna	4 to 6 days

TO REMOVE STAINS FROM WASHABLES

Alcoholic beverages: Pre-soak or sponge fresh stains immediately with cold water, then with cold water and glycerin. Rinse with vinegar for a few seconds if stain remains. These stains may turn brown with age. If wine stain remains, rub with concentrated detergent; wait 15 minutes; rinse. Repeat if necessary. Wash with detergent in hottest water safe for fabric.

Baby Food: Use liquid laundry detergent and brush into stain with an old toothbrush then wash.

Blood: Pre-soak in cold or warm water at least 30 minutes. If stain remains, soak in lukewarm ammonia water (3 tablespoons per gallon water). Rinse. If stain remains, work in detergent, and wash, using bleach safe for fabric.

Candle wax: Use a dull knife to scrape off as much as possible. Place fabric between 2 blotters or facial tissues and press with warm iron. Remove color stain with non-flammable dry cleaning solvent. Wash with detergent in the hottest water safe for fabric.

Chewing gum: Rub area with ice, then scrape off with a dull blade. Sponge with dry cleaning solvent; allow to air dry. Wash in detergent and hottest water safe for fabric.

Chocolate and cocoa: Sponge with club soda.

Coffee: Sponge or soak with cold water as soon as possible. Wash, using detergent and bleach safe for fabric. Remove cream grease stains with non-flammable dry cleaning solvent. Wash again.

Cosmetics: Loosen stain with a non-flammable dry cleaning solvent. Rub detergent in until stain outline is gone. Wash in hottest water and detergent safe for fabric.

Crayon: Scrape with dull blade. Place item between paper towels, press with warm iron. Repeat, only with new paper towels. Wash in hottest water safe for fabric, with detergent and 1 to 2 cups of baking soda. NOTE: If full load is crayon stained, take to cleaners or coin-op dry cleaning machines.

Deodorants: Sponge area with white vinegar. If stain remains, soak with denatured alcohol. Wash with detergent in hottest water safe for fabric.

Dye: If dye transfers from a non-colorfast item during washing, immediately bleach discolored items. Repeat as necessary BEFORE drying. On whites use color remover. CAUTION: Do not use color remover in washer, or around washer and dryer as it may damage the finish.

Egg: Scrape with dull blade. Pre-soak in cold or warm water for at least 30 minutes. Remove grease with dry cleaning solvent. Wash in hottest water safe for fabric, with detergent.

Fruit and fruit juices: Sponge with cold water. Pre-soak in cold or warm water for at least 30 minutes. Wash with detergent and bleach safe for fabric.

Grass: Pre-soak in cold water for at least 30 minutes. Rinse. Pre-treat with detergent, hot water, and bleach safe for fabric. On acetate and colored fabrics, use 1 part of alcohol to 2 parts water.

Grease, oil, tar or butter: Method 1: Use powder or chalk absorbents to remove as much grease as possible. Pre-treat with detergent or non-flammable dry cleaning solvent, or liquid shampoo. Wash in hottest water safe for fabric, using plenty of detergent.

Method 2: Rub spot with lard and sponge with a non-flammable dry cleaning solvent. Wash in hottest water and detergent safe for fabric.

Ink-ball-point pen: Spray with hair spray and launder.

Ketchup or Mustard: Scrape excess. Use commercial spot remover. Rinse; launder.

Liquor: Sponge stain with cool water. Soak in solution of cool water and dishwashing liquid: 30 minutes for light-stain, overnight for heavy. Rinse; launder.

Meat Juices: Scrape with dull blade. Pre-soak in cold or warm water for 30 minutes. Wash with detergent and bleach safe for fabric.

Mildew: Pre-treat as soon as possible with detergent. Wash. If any stain remains, sponge with lemon juice and salt. Dry in sun. Wash, using hottest water, detergent and bleach safe for fabric. NOTE: Mildew is very hard to remove; treat promptly.

Milk, cream, ice cream: Pre-soak in cold or warm water for 30 minutes. Wash. Sponge any grease spots with non-flammable dry cleaning solvent. Wash again.

Mud: Let stain dry. Brush off; launder. Tough stain: Soak in cool water for 30 minutes; work liquid laundry detergent into stain; rinse.

Nail polish: Sponge with acetone-based polish remover or banana oil. Wash. If stain remains, sponge with denatured alcohol to which a few drops of ammonia have been added. Wash again. Do not use polish remover on acetate or triacetate fabrics.

Paint: Oil base: Sponge stains with turpentine, cleaning fluid or paint remover. Pre-treat and wash in hot water. For old stains, sponge with banana oil and then with non-flammable dry cleaning solvent. Wash again.

Water base: Scrape off paint with dull blade. Wash with detergent in water as hot as is safe for fabric.

Perspiration: Sponge fresh stain with ammonia; old stain with vinegar. Pre-soak in cold or warm water. Rinse. Wash in hottest water safe for fabric. If fabric is yellowed, use bleach. If stain still remains, dampen and sprinkle with meat tenderizer, or pepsin. Let stand 1 hour. Brush off and wash. For persistent odor, sponge with colorless mouthwash.

Rust: Soak in lemon juice and salt or oxalic acid solution (3 tablespoons oxalic acid to 1 pint warm water). A commercial rust remover may be used. CAUTION: HANDLE POISONOUS RUST REMOVERS CAREFULLY. KEEP OUT OF REACH OF CHILDREN. NEVER USE OXALIC ACID OR ANY RUST REMOVER AROUND WASHER OR DRYER AS IT CAN DAMAGE THE FINISH. SUCH CHEMICALS MAY ALSO REMOVE PERMANENT PRESS FABRIC FINISHES.

Scorch: Wash with detergent and bleach safe for fabric. On heavier scorching, cover stain with cloth dampened with hydrogen peroxide. Cover this with dry cloth and press with hot iron. Rinse well. CAUTION: Severe scorching cannot be removed because of fabric damage.

Soft drinks: Sponge immediately with cold water and alcohol. Heat and detergent may set stain.

Tea: Sponge or soak with cold water as soon as possible. Wash using detergent and bleach safe for fabric.

STAINS ON CARPETS AND FLOORS

Flatten shag carpets: Raise flattened spots in your carpet where heavy furniture has stood by using a steam iron. Hold the iron over the spot and build up a good steam. Then brush up the carpet.

Candle drippings: For spilled wax on carpet, use a brown paper bag as a blotter and run a hot iron over it, which will absorb the wax.

Dog stains: Blot up excess moisture with paper towel. Pour club soda on the spot and continue blotting. Lay a towel over the spot and set a heavy object on top in order to absorb all the moisture.

Rug care: When washing and drying foam-backed throw rugs, never wash in hot water, and use the "air only" dryer setting to dry. Heat will ruin foam.

Cleaning rugs: If the rug is only slightly dirty, you can clean it with cornmeal. Use a stiff brush to work the cornmeal into the pile of the rug. Take it all out with the vacuum.

Spills on the rug: When spills happen, go to the bathroom and grab a can of shaving cream. Squirt it on the spot then rinse off with water.

Ballpoint ink marks: Saturate the spots with hairspray. Allow to dry. Brush lightly with a solution of water and vinegar.

Glue: Glue can be loosened by saturating the spot with a cloth soaked in vinegar.

Repairing braided rugs: Braided rugs often rip apart. Instead of sewing them, use clear fabric glue to repair. It's that fast and easy.

Repairing a burn: Remove some fuzz from the carpet, either by shaving or pulling out with a tweezer. Roll into the shape of the burn. Apply a good cement glue to the backing of the rug and press the fuzz down into the burned spot. Cover with a piece of cleansing tissue and place a heavy book on top. This will cause the glue to dry very slowly and will get the best results.

Spot remover for outdoor carpeting: Spray spots liberally with a pre-wash commercial spray. Let it set several minutes, then hose down and watch the spots disappear.

Blood on the rug: When you get blood on your rug, rub off as much as you can at first, then take a cloth soaked in cold water and wet the spot, wiping it up as you go. If a little bit remains, pour some ammonia onto the cool, wet cloth and lightly wipe that over the spot, too. Rinse it right away with cold water.

Crayon Marks: Use silver polish to remove from vinyl tile or linoleum.

Spilled nail polish: Allow to almost dry, then peel off of waxed floors or tile.

Tar spots: Use paste wax to remove tar from floors. Works on shoes, too.

Dusting floors: Stretch a nylon stocking over the dust mop. After using, discard the stocking and you will have a clean mop.

Varnished floors: Use cold tea to clean woodwork and varnished floors.

Spilled grease: Rub floor with ice cubes to solidify grease. Scrape up excess and wash with soapy water.

Quick shine: Put a piece of waxed paper under your dust mop. Dirt will stick to the mop and the wax will shine your floors.

Unmarred floors: Put thick old socks over the legs of heavy furniture when moving across floors.

Wood floor care: Never use water or water-based cleaners on wood floors. Over a period of time, warping and swelling will develop.

Floor polisher: When cleaning the felt pads of your floor polisher, place the pads between layers of newspaper and press with an iron to absorb built-up wax.

Garage floors: In an area where a large amount of oil has spilled, lay several thicknesses of newspaper. Saturate the paper with water; press flat against the floor. When dry, remove the newspaper and the spots will have disappeared.

Basement floors: Sprinkle sand on oily spots, let it absorb the oil, and sweep up.

Fix those loose linoleum edges: Take a knife with some tile adhesive and work it under the loose part. Put a heavy weight, such as a big stack of books, over the whole area and keep it weighed down for the amount of time it says on the can of adhesive.

Heel marks: Just take a pencil eraser and wipe them off.

99 WAYS YOU CAN SAVE THE EARTH

1. Buy plain white toilet paper, tissues and paper towels. Dyed paper pollutes.

2. Instead of ammonia-based cleaners, use vinegar and water or baking soda and water.

3. Walk or ride a bike instead of using the

car for short trips.

4. Reuse your grocery bags, or buy a string bag you can carry your groceries in.

5. Buy eggs and milk in cardboard cartons instead of plastic. Or recycle your plastic milk jugs.

6. Take showers instead of baths to save water and energy.

7. Keep your car tires inflated to the proper pressure to improve fuel economy and extend the life of the tires.

8. Don't use electric tools and appliances when hand-operated ones will do the job.

9. Choose a light-colored car with tinted glass to lessen the need for air conditioning.

10. Use mulch and natural ground covers in gardens to contain moisture and conserve water use.

11. Instead of ironing, hang clothes in the bathroom while you shower.

12. Turn off lights in rooms you aren't using.

13. Replace incandescent bulbs with more efficient screw-in compact fluorescent bulbs or fluorescent fixtures.

14. Use high-quality multigrade oil in your car to increase fuel efficiency.

15. Air-dry laundry when possible.

16. Avoid keeping refrigerator or freezer too cold. Government recommended temperature for fresh food is 38 degrees F. For freezers it's 5 degrees F.

17. Reuse aluminum foil and plastic wrap, or avoid them completely by using plastic containers.

18. Plant trees. Strategically located, trees can reduce heating and cooling bills, help prevent soil erosion and reduce air pollution.

19. Water lawns at night to limit evaporation.

20. Compost your leaves and yard waste. You'll improve your garden's soil and avoid sending yard waste to the landfill.

21. Minimize the use of garden chemicals by weeding.

22. Be sure to return your recyclable cans and bottles for your deposit.

23. Don't pour oil and gasoline into the sewer system or on the ground. Take to your local collection site.

24. Buy rechargeable batteries.

25. Use cold water rather than hot water whenever possible for kitchen tasks and laundry.

26. Share rides to work or use public transportation.

27. Buy a fuel-efficient car. Aim for 35 miles per gallon.

28. Read labels and research the products you buy.

29. Don't use excessive amounts of detergent. Presoak dirty laundry.

30. Insulate your basement to save 1/3 on your heat bill.

31. Buy products packaged in recycled paper or cardboard.

32. Caulk and weatherstrip doors and windows.

33. Ask your utility company for an energy audit to assess energy waste in your home.

34. Install water-conserving showerheads and sink-faucet aerators.

35. Insulate your water heater. Turn it down to 121 degrees F.

36. Limit or eliminate your use of "disposable" items.

37. Close off unused areas of your home. Shut off or block heat vents.

38. Compare Energy Guide labels when buying appliances.

39. Keep the fireplace damper closed to prevent heat escape. Keep glass fireplace doors closed when a fire is burning.

40. Use an automatic setback thermostat to turn down heat when you're not home and at night.

41. Capture free solar heat in the winter by opening curtains on south windows during sunny days.

42. Clean lamps and lighting fixtures regularly.

43. Thaw frozen foods in the refrigerator to reduce cooking times and to ensure food safety.

44. Tune up your car regularly for maximum gas mileage.

45. Remove unnecessary items from your car. Each 100 pounds of weight decreases fuel efficiency by 1%.

46. Don't speed; accelerate and slow down gradually.

47. Use latex and other water-based paints instead of toxic enamel or oil-based paints.

48. Repair leaks and drips as soon as they occur. A moderate drip wastes two gallons of water or more per hour.

49. Rent or borrow items you don't often use. Efficient use of products conserves resources.

50. Use small electric pans and ovens to reduce energy use.

51. Run your dishwasher only when full, and use the energy saver cycle.

52. Avoid products made from tropical rainforest woods.

53. Request a Household Hazardous Waste Wheel, showing alternatives to hazardous products, from the Department of Natural Resources, 1-800-DNR-1025 (cost $1.25).

54. For furniture polish, use 1 part lemon juice, 2 parts olive or vegetable oil.

55. For a toilet bowl cleaner, use baking soda and a brush.

56. As a general cleaner, use 1/2 cup borax in 1 gallon water.

57. Instead of chemical air fresheners, set a cotton ball soaked in vanilla extract on a saucer. (Keep away from children and pets.)

58. Instead of toxic mothballs, use cedar chips.

59. Roach killer: mix baking soda and powdered sugar. (Keep away from children and pets.)

60. Ant killer: Use chili powder to hinder entry.

61. Do not toss toxic chemicals into your garbage. Call the Ground-water Hotline 1-800-DNR-1025 to find out how to dispose, or keep them for a Toxic Cleanup Day.

62. Use pump sprays instead of aerosols.

63. Use a holding tank on your boat and don't empty toilet tanks into the water.

64. Don't litter. Pick up any you see, especially plastic rings that can trap birds and fish.

65. Take your own coffee cup to work instead of using disposables.

66. Pour a kettle of boiling water down the drain weekly to melt fat that may be building up.

67. Take old tires to a landfill or processing center for proper disposal.

68. Buy recycled paper, stationery and greeting cards.

69. Shop at your local farmers market. Products are fresh, packaging is minimal and foods are less likely to be made with preservatives.

70. Start an organic garden.

71. Buy in bulk to avoid over packaging.

72. Avoid optional equipment on cars that decreases fuel economy.

73. When having air conditioners serviced, choose companies that will recycle freon instead of venting it.

74. Keep lint screen in dryer clean.

75. Use a trash bag in your car instead of throwing trash out the window.

76. Consider using cloth diapers instead of disposal ones. Check for a local diaper service.

77. Urge your local community to start a curbside recycling program.

78. Start a recycling program where you work. Contact the Department of Natural Resources about the Waste Reduction Assistance Program (WRAP) at 1-800-DNR-1025.

79. Insulate your waterbed by adding an inch of polyethylene foam around the edges and the bottom.

80. To remove rust, rub rust spots briskly with a piece of crumpled aluminum foil, shiny side up.

81. Give leftover paint to theater groups, schools or church groups.

82. Call your local humane society to see if they can use your old newspapers for animal bedding.

83. Check your smoke detector. Put a new battery in if it needs one. Some detectors contain small amounts of low-level radioactive waste. Send used or broken detectors back to the manufacturer.

84. Use equal parts white vinegar and warm water to wash windows or glass. Dry with a soft cloth.

85. Install storm windows.

86. When using hazardous products, use only what is needed. Twice as much does not mean twice the results.

87. Arrange for a waste management presentation for your club or business.

88. Read publications that educate about long-term sustainability.

89. Educate your children about the environment.

90. Write a letter to the editor about your environmental concerns.

91. Get involved in a local treeplanting effort.

92. Learn about global climate change.

93. Join an environmental organization.

94. Research environmental legislation and write to your representatives in the state legislature and in Congress.

95. Think about the kind of Earth you would like to see for your grandchildren's grandchildren.

96. Plan an environmental activity for your club or troop, such as a recycling program.

97. Investigate the environmental record of companies you invest in. Write a letter as a shareholder to the company president or sell your stock.

98. Talk to friends, relatives and co-workers about the environment.

99. Copy this list and send it to your friends.

PLANTS

• Always choose a pot that's not more than two inches larger in diameter than the old pot.

• Blooming plants should be repotted after they're done blossoming, not before.

• To help reduce the shock of repotting, give the new soil a thorough watering.

• Clay pots should be soaked in water for a few minutes before you repot your plants. This prevents the clay from absorbing moisture from the potting soil.

• Fill a string mesh bag with suet and scraps of leftover food and hang from a tree limb for those cheery winter birds.

• After holidays–remove branches from the Christmas tree and put them over flower beds for insulation.

• Take old Christmas tree outside and stabilize in the ground. Hang grapefruit and orange cups from the branches with wire and fill cups with bird seed for the birdies.

• When you start seeds indoors, it's best to plant them in a small amount of dirt at first. Gradually add more dirt as the plant grows. Do this and your plants will be much stronger and do better after you set them outside.

• If you have a large garden, but not a lot of time to weed, put two layers of newspaper between your rows. This keeps the weeds down and saves you a lot of time.

• Plant pole beans next to sunflowers. The beans will climb the lower part of the sunflowers and you won't need any poles.

• Your African Violets will bloom longer, prettier and more abundantly if you stick a few rusty nails in the soil alongside them.